POPULAR WILDFLOWERS

of the

Canadian

Prairies

NEIL L. JENNINGS

RMB

This book is dedicated to our dear friend Carol Baker, whose cheerfulness, class and pluck in the face of seemingly insurmountable adversity stand as an inspiration to all of us. Still sorely missed after all this time.

For information on purchasing bulk quantities of this book, or to
obtain media excerpts or invite the author to speak at an event,
please visit rmbooks.com and select the "Contact" tab.

RMB | Rocky Mountain Books Ltd.
rmbooks.com
@rmbooks
facebook.com/rmbooks

Cataloguing data available from Library and Archives Canada
ISBN 9781771603515 (paperback)
ISBN 9781771603522 (electronic)

All photographs are by the author unless otherwise noted.

Printed and bound in Canada

We would like to also take this opportunity to acknowledge the traditional territories
upon which we live and work. In Calgary, Alberta, we acknowledge the Niitsitapi
(Blackfoot) and the people of the Treaty 7 region in Southern Alberta, which includes
the Siksika, the Piikuni, the Kainai, the Tsuut'ina and the Stoney Nakoda First Nations,
including Chiniki, Bearpaw, and Wesley First Nations. The City of Calgary is also home
to Métis Nation of Alberta, Region III. In Victoria, British Columbia, we acknowledge the
traditional territories of the Lkwungen (Esquimalt, and Songhees), Malahat, Pacheedaht,
Scia'new, T'Sou-ke and W̱SÁNEĆ (Pauquachin, Tsartlip, Tsawout, Tseycum) peoples.

We acknowledge the financial support of the Government of Canada through the Canada
Book Fund and the Canada Council for the Arts, and of the province of British Columbia
through the British Columbia Arts Council and the Book Publishing Tax Credit.

Disclaimer
It is up to the users of this guidebook to acquire the necessary skills for safe experiences
and to exercise caution. The author and publisher of this guide accept no responsibility for
your actions or the results that occur from another's actions, choices, or judgments. If you
have any doubt as to the safety of any given plant, avoidance is the best course of action.

CONTENTS

ACKNOWLEDGEMENTS

I owe a debt of gratitude to a number of family members who contributed to this book by their continuous encouragement and support. Particular appreciation goes to my wife, Linda, who accompanied me on many flower outings and allowed me frequent absences from other duties in favour of chasing blooming flowers. My children, and, I am happy to say, their children, all deserve mention as well, given that they were often seconded to tramp around with me and bring me home alive. Thanks also go to many friends who encouraged me in my projects and often went into the field with me, according me a level of patience that was above and beyond the call of duty. I also wish to especially thank (or perhaps blame) the now departed S. Don Cahoon, who often shamed me with my ignorance and convinced me to educate myself about the beauty that resides in fields of wildflowers.

INTRODUCTION

This book is intended to be a field guide for the amateur naturalist to the identification of wild flowering plants commonly found in the prairie environments of western Canada and several of the border states of the USA. This is not a book for scientists. It is for the curious traveller who wants to become acquainted with the flowers encountered during outings. The book differs from most other field guides in that it makes no assumption that the reader has any background in things botanical. It is also small enough to actually carry in the field and not be a burden. I believe most people want to be able to identify the flowers they encounter because this enriches their outdoor experience. Some might think it a difficult skill to perfect, but take heart and consider this: you can easily put names and faces together for several hundred family members, friends, acquaintances, movie stars, authors, business and world leaders, sports figures etc. Wildflower recognition is no different, and it need not be complicated.

The book does not cover all of the species of wildflowers and flowering shrubs that exist here, but it does include a large representation of the more common floral communities that might be encountered in a typical day during blooming season. No book that I am acquainted with covers all species in any region, and indeed if such a source existed, it would be too large to be easily carried. Obviously, space will not permit a discussion of all such species, nor would it be pertinent for the amateur naturalist.

"Do you know what this flower is called?" is one of the most often asked questions when I meet people in the field. Hopefully, this book will enable the user to answer this question. Identification of the unknown species is based on comparison of the unknown plant with the photographs contained in the book, augmented by the narrative descriptions associated with the species pictured. In many instances the exact species will be apparent, while in other cases the reader will be led to plants that are similar to the unknown plant, thus providing a starting point for further investigation. For the purposes of this book, scientific jargon has been kept to a minimum. I have set out to produce the best photographic representations I could obtain, together with some information about the plant that the reader might find interesting, and that might assist the reader in remembering the names of the plants. In my view, what most people really want to know about wildflowers is "what is this thing?" and "tell me something interesting about it." Botanical detail, while interesting and enlightening to some of us, will turn off many people.

The plants depicted in the book are arranged first by colour and then by family. This is a logical arrangement for the non-botanist because the first thing a person notes about a flower is its colour. All of the plants shown in the book are identified by their prevailing common names. Where I knew of other common names applied to any plant, I have noted them. I have also included the scientific names of the plants. This inclusion is made to promote specificity. Common names vary significantly from one geographic region to another, but scientific names do not. If you want to learn the scientific names of the plants to promote precision, that's fine. If not, no worries, but just be mindful that many plants have different common names applied to them depending on geography and local usage.

A few cautionary comments and suggestions:

While you are outdoors, go carefully among the plants so as not to damage or disturb them. Stay on the established trails; those trails exist to allow us to view the natural environment without trampling it to death. Many environments are delicate and can be significantly damaged by indiscriminately tromping around in the flora.

Do not pick the flowers. Leave them for others to enjoy.

Do not attempt to transplant wild plants. Such attempts are most often doomed to failure.

Do not eat any plants or plant parts. Do not attempt to use any plants or plant parts for medicinal purposes. To do so presents a potentially significant health hazard. Many of the plants are poisonous – some violently so.

One final cautionary note: the pursuit of wildflowers can be addictive, though not hazardous to your health.

Neil L. Jennings
Calgary, Alberta

TERRITORIAL RANGE OF
WILDFLOWERS

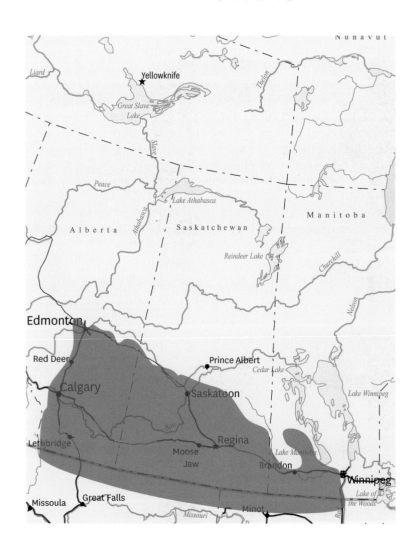

Red, Orange *and* Pink Flowers

This section includes flowers that are red, orange or pink when encountered in the field. Flowers that are pinkish often can have tones running to lavender, though, so if you do not find the one you are looking for here, check the Blue/Purple section.

Common Hound's-Tongue
Cynoglossum officinale

BORAGE FAMILY

This course, hairy biennial weed was introduced from Europe and grows in disturbed ground and roadside ditches. It has a single leafy stem that grows to 80 cm tall. The leaves are alternate, elliptical to lance-shaped, tapered to slender stalks at the base of the plant and becoming stalkless and clasping near the top of the plant. The flowers appear from the upper leaf axils and are reddish-purple and funnel-shaped. The fruits are clusters of small nutlets that are covered with barbed prickles that catch on clothing and fur, a mechanism for seed dispersal.

Water Smartweed (Water Knotweed)
Polygonum amphibium

BUCKWHEAT FAMILY

This plant occurs from prairie to subalpine elevations, and is found in ponds, marshes and ditches and along lakeshores, often forming mats in standing water. The plant may grow on land adjacent to or in water. The leaves are large, oblong to lance-shaped, rounded or pointed at the tips, and have a prominent mid-vein. The flowers are pink and occur in a dense, oblong cluster at the top of thick, smooth stalks. The plant was used by Indigenous peoples both medicinally in poultices to treat piles and skin disease, and as food. The plant is also food for a large variety of birds.

Red Columbine (Western Columbine)

Aquilegia formosa

BUTTERCUP FAMILY

These beautiful flowers are found in meadows and dry to moist woods, and are among the showiest of all western wildflowers. The leaves of the plant are mostly basal and compound, with three sets of three leaflets each. The flowers occur on stems above the basal leaves, and are composed of five yellow petal blades and five red sepals with straight spurs at their ends. The leaves on the flowering stem are considerably smaller than the basal leaves, appearing with only three leaflets each. Numerous stamens extend well beyond the petals.

Cushion Cactus (Ball Cactus)

Coryphantha vivipara
(also *Escobaria vivipara*)

CACTUS FAMILY

This squat, low-growing perennial cactus grows singly or in clumps in dry, eroded, sandy and rocky soils, often on south-facing slopes in the southern part of the area. Its pin-cushion stem rises only a few inches above the ground. The whole surface of the rounded stem is covered with evenly spaced, spine-tipped projections. The beautiful purplish to pink flowers are short-lived and have numerous lance-shaped petals and a shower of yellow stamens.

Dotted Blazingstar

Liatris punctata

COMPOSITE FAMILY

This plant is a showy perennial that grows to 60 cm tall from a thickened rootstock, often forming clumps in dry grasslands, meadows and hillsides in the southern prairies. The grey-green leaves are numerous, alternate, narrowly lance-shaped and entire, and have a prominent whitish mid-vein. The leaves are somewhat covered with translucent glandular dots or pits. The flowers are rose coloured to deep purple, and they are arranged in a dense, crowded cluster bunched at the top of the flowering stem.

Flodman's Thistle

Cirsium flodmanii

COMPOSITE FAMILY

This perennial native thistle grows from a sturdy taproot in coulees and at the bases of hills, and can reach up to 1 m tall. The plant is covered in woolly hairs, giving it a white-mottled appearance. The basal leaves are up to 15 cm long, while the stem leaves are shorter. The leaves are greenish above, grey woolly beneath, deeply incised and covered with spines. The plant bears one to five large flower heads, purple in colour and up to 5 cm wide.

Spotted Knapweed
Centaurea maculosa

COMPOSITE FAMILY

This introduced noxious weed inhabits roadsides, ditches and disturbed areas, and has become a problem in many locales. The plant is many-branched and grows to more than a metre tall from creeping rhizomes. The flowers are heads at the ends of branches, with dark pink or purple disc florets only. The name Knapweed is derived from the ancient English *knap*, meaning "knob" or "bump," a reference to the bumps on the branches of the plant. It is believed that this plant was inadvertently introduced into North America when its seeds contaminated a shipment of forage crop seed.

Black Gooseberry
Ribes lacustre

CURRANT FAMILY

This erect deciduous shrub grows to 150 cm tall in moist woods and open areas. The branches of the plant have small prickles and stout thorns at leaf and branch bases. The leaves are alternate and shaped like maple leaves, with three to five deeply cut palmate lobes. The reddish, saucer-shaped flowers hang in elongated clusters. The fruits are dark purple to black berries that bristle with tiny hairs. The genus *Ribes* includes all Currants and Gooseberries. Gooseberries are bristly hairy, while Currants are not.

Fireweed (Great Willowherb)

Chamaenerion angustifolium (form. *Epilobium angustifolium*)

EVENING PRIMROSE FAMILY

This plant occurs along roadsides and in disturbed areas, clearings and shaded woods from low elevations to the subalpine zone. It is often one of the first plants to appear after a fire. The pink, four-petalled flowers bloom in long terminal clusters. Bracts between the petals are narrow. The flowers bloom from the bottom of the cluster first, then upward on the stem. The leaves are alternate and appear whorled. Fireweed is the floral emblem of the Yukon.

Scarlet Butterflyweed

Gaura coccinea

EVENING PRIMROSE FAMILY

This is a plant of grasslands and dry south-facing slopes. The flowers are whitish when they first bloom, becoming scarlet or pink as the flower ages. Usually only a few of the flowers on an individual plant bloom at once, and the flowers open fully only at night. The specific epithet, *coccinea*, means "scarlet," a reference to the colour of the flower. The common name arises most probably because the flowers are said to be shaped like butterflies.

Elephant's Head
Pedicularis groenlandica

FIGWORT FAMILY

This is a plant of wet meadows, stream banks and wetland margins. Its flowers appear in dense clusters atop a substantial stalk that can grow to 50 cm tall. Each of the flowers is reddish-purple to pinkish, and has an uncanny resemblance to an elephant's head, with a curved trunk and flared ears.

All members of this genus are somewhat parasitic on the roots of other plants, so transplantation is doomed to failure. When encountered, a close examination of this delightful flower is recommended, but be careful of the fragile habitat in which it lives.

Red Paintbrush
Castilleja miniata

FIGWORT FAMILY

A plant of alpine meadows, well-drained slopes, open subalpine forests, moist stream banks and open foothills woods, Paintbrush is widely distributed and extremely variable in colour. The leaves are narrow and sharp-pointed, linear to lance-shaped and usually without teeth or divisions, but sometimes the upper leaves have three shallow lobes. The showy red, leafy bracts, which are actually modified leaves, resemble a brush dipped in paint, hence the common name.

Strawberry Blite

Chenopodium capitatum

GOOSEFOOT FAMILY

This plant is found from valley to subalpine elevations and is distinctive for its large triangular or arrowhead-shaped leaves and its dense, fleshy clusters of bright-red flowers. The flower clusters appear at the ends of branches on the plant, usually in interrupted bunches and in the leaf axils. The leaves are rich in vitamins and minerals and are said to taste like spinach. The flowers too are edible, though most authorities warn against over-indulging in consuming the plant. Some Indigenous peoples used the red flowers as a source of dye, prompting the common name Indian Paint.

Kinnikinnick (Bearberry)

Arctostaphylos uva-ursi

HEATH FAMILY

This trailing or matted evergreen shrub grows low to the ground and has long branches with reddish, flaky bark and shiny green, leathery leaves. The flowers are pale pink and urn-shaped, appearing in clumps at the ends of the stems. The fruits are dull-red berries that apparently are relished by bears and birds, though they tend to seem dry and mealy to humans. They are edible, however, and have been prepared in a variety of ways. "Kinnikinnick" is believed to be of Algonquin origin and means "something to smoke," a reference to the use of the leaves of the plant as a tobacco.

Pine-Drops

Pterospora andromedea

HEATH FAMILY

Pine-Drops is a rare saprophyte, a plant that gets its nutrients from decaying plant or animal matter. It grows to 1 m tall in deep humus of coniferous or mixed woods. The leaves are mostly basal and resemble scales. The flowers are cream-coloured to yellowish, and occur in a raceme that covers roughly the top half of the stalk. The petals are united into an urn shape, and hang downward off bent flower stalks, like small lanterns. The stalks of the plant will remain erect for a year or more after the plant dies.

Pink Wintergreen

Pyrola asarifolia

HEATH FAMILY

This plant is an erect perennial that inhabits moist to dry coniferous and mixed forests and riverine environments from the montane to the subalpine zone. Its waxy, pale-pink to purplish-red nodding flowers are shaped like an inverted cup or bell and have a long, curved, projecting style. The leaves are basal in a rosette, have a leathery appearance, and are shiny, rounded and dark green. The name "wintergreen" refers to evergreen leaves, not the flavour that has the same name.

Pipsissewa (Prince's Pine)

Chimaphila umbellata

HEATH FAMILY

This small evergreen shrub grows to 30 cm tall in coniferous woods. Its glossy, dark-green leaves are narrowly spoon-shaped and saw-toothed, and occur in whorls. The waxy pink flowers are saucer-shaped and nodding on an erect stem above the leaves. The fruits of the plant are dry, round, brown capsules that often overwinter on the stem. "Pipsissewa" is an adaptation of the Cree name for the plant.

Nodding Onion

Allium cernuum

LILY FAMILY

This plant is common in the region, and is easily identified by its smooth, leafless stem and drooping or nodding pink inflorescence. There are usually 8–12 flowers in the nodding cluster. The stem gives off a strong oniony odour when crushed. Indigenous peoples consumed the bulbs, both raw and cooked and as flavouring for other foods, and dried them for later use.

Western Wood Lily
Lilium philadelphicum

LILY FAMILY

This lily grows in moist meadows, in dense to open woods and at the edges of aspen groves, from prairie elevations to the low subalpine zone. The leaves are numerous, lance-shaped, smooth and alternate on the stem, except for the upper leaves, which are in whorls. Each plant may produce from one to five bright-orange to orange-red flowers, each with three virtually identical sepals and petals. This plant is often confused with the Columbia Lily (*L. columbianum*), which is coloured similarly, but the tepals on the Columbia Lily are reflexed, while the petals on the Wood Lily are held in a chalice shape.

Scarlet Mallow
Sphaeralcea coccinea

MALLOW FAMILY

This low-growing perennial stands up to 20 cm tall and may appear singly or in large colonies. It grows from a thick, branched, scaly, woody rootstock, and occurs along roadsides, railway rights-of-way and other disturbed places as well as in grasslands. The leafy stems are prostrate and spread out from the woody base to end in dense clusters of red flowers. The leaves are alternate and long-stalked, with several divisions and notches at the tips. The stems and leaves are covered with star-shaped clusters of fine white hair, giving the whole plant a greyish-green appearance. The flowers are shaped like Hollyhocks.

Showy Milkweed

Asclepias speciosa

MILKWEED FAMILY

This perennial plant is rather spectacular with its tall, coarse stem, large leaves and round clusters of pink to purple flowers. It grows up to 2 m tall from a thick, creeping rootstock, often occurring in clumps. It is found in moist grasslands and thickets and along roadsides and streams. Its thick, dark-green leaves are opposite, short-stalked, oblong or oval, prominently veined, and rounded at the tip, sometimes having a sharp spine. The flowers have a strong scent and occur in dense, rounded, umbrella-shaped clusters that can span 7 cm across.

Spotted Coralroot (Summer Coralroot)

Corallorhiza maculata

ORCHID FAMILY

A plant of moist woods and bogs, this orchid grows from extensive coral-like rhizomes. There are no leaves, but the plant has several membranous bracts that sheathe the purplish to brownish stem. A number of flowers appear on each stem, loosely arranged up the stem in a raceme. The three sepals and two upper petals are reddish purple. The lip petal is white with dark-red or purple spots and two lateral lobes. The plant lacks chlorophyll and does not produce food by photosynthesis, relying instead on parasitizing fungi in the soil.

Striped Coralroot

Corallorhiza striata

ORCHID FAMILY

This orchid grows from extensive coral-like rhizomes, and occurs in moist woods and bogs in the montane and subalpine zones. The pink to yellowish-pink flowers have purplish stripes on the sepals, and the lowest petal forms a tongue-shaped lip. A number of flowers appear on each stem, loosely arranged up the stem in an unbranched raceme. The leaves are tubular sheaths that surround, and somewhat conceal, the base of the purplish stem. The plant depends on a complex relationship with fungi in the soil for germination and survival.

Wild Bergamot

Monarda fistulosa

MINT FAMILY

This showy flower inhabits grasslands and open woods, blooming in the summer months. The stems of the plant are erect and square, and have a strong and distinctive odour of mint. The stem is topped with a dense cluster of pink to violet flowers. The leaves are opposite, triangular to ovate, and pointed at the ends. Some Indigenous peoples used the plant as a perfume, meat preservative and insect repellent. It is also reported that the plant was used ceremonially in the Sun Dance.

Red Clover

Trifolium pratense

PEA FAMILY

A European species now well established in North America, this plant grows to 60 cm tall at low to mid-elevations. Its leaves are in threes, often displaying a white, crescent-shaped spot near the base. The pinkish to purple flowers are pea-like, and up to 200 of them occur in dense heads 2–3 cm in diameter at stem tops. Two leaves lie immediately below the flower head. The name "clover" is derived from the Latin *clava*, which means "club."

Pitcherplant

Sarracenia purpurea

PITCHERPLANT FAMILY

This unique and unusual species can be found in the prairie provinces in northern boreal forest regions. The plant is carnivorous and grows in sedge fens and bogs. Its evergreen leaves are arranged in a basal rosette which has been modified to form a pitcher that stands up to 30 cm tall. The "spout" of the pitcher is upright, and the leaves forming the vessel have strong, red venation. The pitcher holds water, and when a hapless visitor falls into the pitcher, the plant digests it. Other locally common names are Flytrap, Indian Jug and Frog's Britches.

Prickly Rose

Rosa acicularis

ROSE FAMILY

This is a deciduous shrub that grows up to 150 cm tall, with freely branched stems, and thorns at the base of each leaf. The flowers are pink with five broad petals. Leaves are oblong, notched and somewhat hairy beneath roadsides. The Prickly Rose will easily hybridize with other members of the rose family, and the hybrids can be difficult to identify specifically. The dark-red fruits are fleshy, round to oval hips with sepals remaining on top, like a beard. They are rich in vitamin C, and can be used to make a delicious jelly.

Three-Flowered Avens (Old Man's Whiskers)

Geum triflorum

ROSE FAMILY

This plant is widespread on dry plateaus and in arid basins and open grasslands from prairies to subalpine elevations. The dull purplish to pinkish hairy flowers bloom in early spring, nodding at the top of the stem, usually in clusters of three though some plants can have as many as five on a single stem. The flowers remain semi-closed and do not open completely the way many common flowers do. The fruits are feathery clusters of brownish to purplish, plume-like achenes (small, dry, one-seeded fruits) that are sown by wind action. Indeed, when these seeds were being blown by the wind many early settlers referred to the phenomenon as "prairie smoke," accounting for another common name for the species.

White, Green *and* Brown Flowers

This section includes flowers that are predominantly white or cream-coloured, green or brown when encountered in the field. Given that some flowers fade to other colours as they age, if you do not find the one you are looking for here, check the other parts of the book.

Evening Star

Mentzelia decapetala

BLAZING STAR FAMILY

This stout, leafy, branched biennial grows up to 90 cm tall and appears on exposed clay hillsides and in eroded badlands in the prairies. Its sharp-toothed leaves are alternate, prominently veined, and roughened with thick, whitish hairs. The large flowers appear at the terminal ends of the branches. The white flowers are showy, and have five sepals and ten pointed petals. There are numerous yellow stamens. The flowers open in the evening and bloom during the night, hence the name Evening Star. The plant uses moths as pollinators.

Clustered Oreocarya

Cryptantha nubigena

BORAGE FAMILY

This plant is densely covered with bristly white hairs, and occurs on dry hillsides and in prairie habitats. The lower leaves are spoon-shaped with rounded to pointed tips, while the upper leaves are linear. The small white flowers appear in clusters in the axils of the leaves on the upper two-thirds of the erect stem. The pleasantly scented flowers are funnel-shaped and five-parted, with yellow centres. They bloom early in the spring.

Water Crowfoot (Water Buttercup)

Ranunculus aquatilis

BUTTERCUP FAMILY

This aquatic Buttercup lives in ponds, lakes, ditches and slow-moving streams. The white flowers have five sepals, five to ten petals and numerous pistils and stamens. The plant has two types of leaves. The submerged leaves are matting, thread-like filaments, while the floating leaves are deeply cleft into three to five lobes. The flowers are flecked with gold at the base, and are buoyed above the water on short stems. Yellow Water Crowfoot, which has yellow petals, is now considered to be in the same species.

Baneberry

Actaea rubra

BUTTERCUP FAMILY

This perennial grows up to 1 m tall in moist, shady woods and thickets, along streams and in clearings from low to subalpine elevations. The plant has one to several stout, upright, branching stems. Its coarse-toothed leaves are all on the stem and are divided two or three times into threes. The inflorescence is a dense, white, cone-shaped cluster of flowers that appears on top of a spike. The fruit is a large cluster of either shiny red or white berries. The leaves, roots and berries of this plant are extremely poisonous.

Canada Anemone

Anemone canadensis

BUTTERCUP FAMILY

This is a plant of moist grasslands and woods, aspen groves and riverine thickets. The leaves are toothed and deeply divided into three to five lobes on long leaf stalks. The leaves are light green, with fine hairs above and below. They are long-veined and attached to the stem in a whorl. The flowers are composed of five white, petal-like sepals that are rounded at the tip, with soft hairs underneath. The genus name is said to be derived from the Greek word *anemos*, which means "wind," a reference to the wind being the seed distribution mechanism.

Western Clematis (White Virgin's Bower)

Clematis ligusticifolia

BUTTERCUP FAMILY

This plant is a climbing or trailing woody vine that occurs in coulees, creek bottoms and river valleys. It clings to and climbs over other plants by a twist or kink in its leaf stalks. Its leaves are opposite and compound, with five to seven long-stalked leaflets. The flowers are white and borne in dense clusters. The flowers are unisexual. The male flowers have many stamens but no pistils, while the female ones have both pistils and sterile stamens.

Windflower
Anemone multifida
BUTTERCUP FAMILY

This plant favours south-facing slopes, grasslands and open woods. Like all anemones, Windflowers possess no petals, only sepals. The flowers are a variety of colours, from white to yellowish to red, and appear atop a woolly stem. Beneath the flowers are bract-like leaves attached directly to the stem. The leaves are palmate, with deeply incised, silky-haired leaflets somewhat reminiscent of poppy leaves. The fruits are achenes in a rounded head, which later form a large, cottony mass. The common name, Windflower, comes from the method of distributing the long-plumed seeds of the plant

Cow Parsnip
Heracleum lanatum
CARROT FAMILY

A denizen of shaded riverine habitat, stream banks, seeps and moist open woods, this plant grows over 2 m tall. The flowers are distinctive in large, compound, umbrella-shaped clusters (umbels) composed of numerous white flowers, with petals in fives. The leaves, compound in threes, are usually very large, softly hairy, toothed and deeply lobed.

Water Hemlock

Cicuta maculata
(also *C. douglasii*)

CARROT FAMILY

This is a plant of marshes, river and stream banks and low, wet areas. It produces several large umbrella-like clusters (compound umbels) of white flowers appearing at the top of a sturdy stalk. The leaves are alternate and twice compound, with many lance-shaped leaflets. The primary lateral veins in the leaves end between the notched teeth on the leaflets rather than at their points. This is unique, and separates this species from parsley family members in the area.

While lovely to look at, the Water Hemlock is considered to be perhaps the most poisonous plant in North America. All parts of the plant are toxic, as testified to by several of its common names, including Children's Bane, Beaver Poison and Death of Man.

Common Cattail

Typha latifolia

CATTAIL FAMILY

This plant is very common in the area and is well recognized on slough and pond margins and along streams. Its leaves are long, flat and strap-like, and the unisexual flowers are dense, cylindrical flower masses. The top of the mass consists of the pollen-bearing male flowers, while the bottom holds the tightly packed pistillate flowers. Indigenous peoples made extensive use of Cattails. The leaves were woven into mats, hats, bags and even capes; the seed heads were used as an absorbent in diapers, as well as for stuffing in mattresses and pillows; and the young flowers and rhizomes were eaten.

Arrow-Leaved Sweet Coltsfoot

Petasites sagittatus

COMPOSITE FAMILY

This plant occurs from low to subalpine elevations in wetlands, ditches and slough margins, sometimes appearing in standing water. The large, long-stalked basal leaves are triangular to heart-shaped with toothed margins and are densely white-woolly underneath. The flowering stems appear before the basal leaves do. The stem does not have leaves, but does have some overlapping bracts. The inflorescence is a cluster of composite heads sitting atop the stem. The flowers consist almost entirely of whitish disc flowers, sometimes with a few white ray flowers.

Ox-Eye Daisy

Leucanthemum vulgare

COMPOSITE FAMILY

An invasive Eurasian perennial from a well-developed rhizome, this plant frequents low to mid-elevations in moist to moderately dry sites such as roadsides, clearings, pastures and disturbed areas. The flowers are solitary composite heads at the ends of branches, with white ray flowers and yellow disc flowers. The basal leaves are broadly lance-shaped or narrowly spoon-shaped. The stem leaves are oblong and smaller. This species is very prolific and will overgrow large areas if not kept in check. Many people consider it the most common and recognizable wildflower in North America.

Pineapple Weed (Disc Mayweed)

Matricaria discoidea

COMPOSITE FAMILY

This branching annual grows up to 40 cm tall along roadsides, in ditches and on disturbed ground. The stem leaves are alternate and fern-like, with finely dissected, narrow segments. Basal leaves have usually fallen off by the time flowering occurs. The flowers are several to many composite heads, with greenish to yellow disc florets on a cone- or dome-shaped base. There are no ray florets. When crushed, the leaves and flowers of the plant produce a distinctive pineapple aroma, hence the common name.

Tufted Fleabane

Erigeron caespitosus

COMPOSITE FAMILY

A plant of dry, open places, south-facing slopes, coulees and eroded badlands, this small, white, daisy-like flower can grow in large bunches or clusters. The ray florets are usually white but sometimes bluish or pink. The numerous narrow petals surround central yellow disc florets. The grey-green basal leaves are short, hairy and lance- or spoon-shaped.

Yarrow

Achillea millefolium

COMPOSITE FAMILY

This is a plant of dry to moist grasslands, open riverine forests, aspen woods and disturbed areas. The individual white flower heads appear in a dense, flat-topped or rounded terminal cluster. The ray florets are white to cream coloured (sometimes pink), and the central disc florets are straw coloured. The leaves are woolly, greyish to blue-green and finely divided, almost resembling a fern. Yarrow can occur in large colonies. The genus name, *Achillea*, is in honour of Achilles, the Greek warrior.

Northern Gooseberry

Ribes oxyacanthoides

CURRANT FAMILY

This plant is an erect or sprawling deciduous shrub that grows up to 90 cm tall and occurs in moist woods, thickets and open areas. The branches of the plant are covered with small prickles and also have stout spines up to 1 cm long at the branch nodes. The leaves are alternate and shaped like maple leaves, with three to five palmate lobes. The white to greenish-yellow flowers are tubular in shape, with five erect petals and five larger, spreading sepals, and bloom from the leaf axils in the early spring. The fruits are smooth bluish-purple berries up to 1 cm in diameter.

Spreading Dogbane

Apocynum androsaemifolium

DOGBANE FAMILY

This relatively common shrub occurs in thickets and wooded areas, and has freely branching, slender stems. The egg-shaped leaves are opposite and have sharp-pointed tips. The small, white to light pinkish, bell-shaped flowers droop from the ends of the leafy stems, usually in clusters. The petal lobes are spreading and bent back, usually with dark-pink veins. Indigenous peoples used the tough fibres from these plants to fashion strong thread for making items like bowstrings and fishing nets. The pods of the plant are poisonous to eat.

Bunchberry (Dwarf Dogwood)

Cornus canadensis

DOGWOOD FAMILY

This is a plant of moist coniferous woods, often found on rotting logs and stumps. The flowers are clusters of inconspicuous greenish-white flowers set among four white, petal-like showy bracts. The leaves are in a terminal whorl of four to seven, all prominently veined, and are dark green above, lighter underneath. The fruits are bright-red berries. The plant's common name, Bunchberry, is probably derived from the fact that the fruits are all bunched together in a terminal cluster when ripe.

Red Osier Dogwood

Cornus stolonifera

DOGWOOD FAMILY

This willow-like shrub that grows up to 3 m high, often forms impenetrable thickets along streams and in moist forests. The reddish bark is quite distinctive, and it becomes even redder with the advent of frosts. The leaves are heavily veined, dark green above and pale underneath. The small, greenish-white flowers occur in a flat-topped cluster at the terminal ends of stems. The fruits are small white berries, appearing in clumps. This plant is extremely important winter browse for moose.

Butte Primrose (Gumbo Evening Primrose)

Oenothera caespitosa

EVENING PRIMROSE FAMILY

This low-growing, tufted perennial grows from a woody root and is found on dry clay slopes, eroded prairie and roadcuts. The leaves are basal, entire, spoon- to lance-shaped, wavy-margined, prominently mid-veined and irregularly toothed. They occur in a rosette on the ground, and may have a reddish tinge. The sweet-scented flowers are showy and white, with four large, shallowly lobed petals and four sepals that are often reflexed and pale pink. The flowers are short-lived, and become pinker as they age.

Wild Sarsaparilla

Aralia nudicaulis

GINSENG FAMILY

This plant prefers the dark woods of moist montane forests. Its leaves are up to 50 cm long, arising singly from an underground stem. Each leaf has a long, bare stalk that terminates in three to five leaflets. The leaflets are up to 15 cm long, and are sharp-toothed and pointed at the ends. The flowers arise from a short stem near ground level, well below the spreading leaflets. The tiny, whitish-green flowers are arranged in three round umbels.

Fringed Grass of Parnassus

Parnassia fimbriata

GRASS OF PARNASSUS FAMILY

These plants abound in riverine habitat, pond edges and boggy places from the montane to the subalpine. The white flowers are very delicate looking. The flowers appear as singles on a slender stem, with five white petals and greenish or yellowish veins. The lower edges of the petals are fringed with hairs. Alternating fertile and sterile stamens are characteristic of this genus. The leaves are mostly basal and broadly kidney-shaped. A single leaf clasps the flowering stem about halfway up.

Greenish-Flowered Wintergreen (Green Wintergreen)

Pyrola chlorantha

HEATH FAMILY

This is an erect perennial that inhabits riverine environments and moist to dry coniferous and mixed forests from montane to subalpine zones. Its flowers have five waxy, greenish-white petals and a long style attached to a prominent ovary. The bell-shaped flowers are distributed on short stalks up the main stem. The shiny, rounded, dark-green leaves are evergreen, basal in a rosette and have a leathery appearance.

Indian Pipe (Ghost Plant)

Monotropa uniflora

HEATH FAMILY

This unique and unusual sapro-phyte grows either solitary or in clumps from a dense root system, and occurs in moist, shaded woods in rich soil. It is fairly rare, and is said to appear almost overnight, like a mushroom. Instead of leaves, it has colourless scales. The flowers are white to cream-coloured, nodding on stems up to 20 cm tall and shaped like a smoking pipe stuck into the ground by the stem. The flowers darken to black with age and turn upward at the top of the stem. Stems from the previous year's growth may persist.

Labrador Tea

Ledum groenlandicum

HEATH FAMILY

This much-branched evergreen shrub is widespread in low to sub-alpine elevations in peaty wetlands and moist coniferous forests. The flowers are white and numerous, with 5–10 protruding stamens in umbrella-like clusters at the ends of branches. The leaves are alter-nate and narrow, with edges rolled under. They are deep green and leathery on top, with dense rusty hairs under-neath. The fresh or dried leaves can be brewed into an aromatic tea, hence the common name. They were also used in barns to drive away mice and in houses to repel fleas.

One-Sided Wintergreen

Pyrola secunda
(also *Orthilia secunda*)

HEATH FAMILY

This small forest dweller grows up to 15 cm tall at low to subalpine elevations in dry to moist coniferous or mixed woods and clearings. The white to yellowish-green flowers lie on one side of the arching stalk, arranged in a raceme of six to ten and sometimes more. The flowers resemble small street lights strung along a curving pole. The straight style sticks out beyond the petals, with a flat, five-lobed stigma. The egg-shaped, evergreen leaves are basal and fine-toothed at their margins. Once seen, this lovely little flower is unmistakable in the woods.

Single Delight (One-Flowered Wintergreen)

Moneses uniflora

HEATH FAMILY

This intriguing little plant inhabits damp forests, usually on rotting wood. It is quite tiny, standing only 15 cm tall, and its single white flower, open and nodding at the top of the stem, is less than 5 cm in diameter. The flower looks like a small white umbrella offering shade. The leaves are basal, oval and evergreen, attached to the base of the stem. The style is prominent and tipped with a five-lobed stigma that almost looks like a mechanical part of some kind. The plant is also known locally as Wood Nymph and Shy Maiden.

Low-Bush Cranberry (Mooseberry)

Viburnum edule

HONEYSUCKLE FAMILY

This plant is a sprawling deciduous shrub that grows to heights of up to 2 m in moist to wet forests, along streams and in boggy areas from low to subalpine elevations. The leaves are opposite, sharp-toothed and maple-leaf-shaped with three lobes. The tiny, white, five-parted flowers appear in flat-topped showy clusters between leaves along the stem. The fruits are clusters of red or orange berries that contain a large, flat stone. The fruits remain on the plant after the leaves fall, and the overripe berries and decaying leaves often produce a musty odour in the woods.

Snowberry

Symphoricarpos albus

HONEYSUCKLE FAMILY

This common deciduous shrub occurs from coast to coast in North America, and is found in well-drained, open or wooded sites from prairies to lower subalpine zones. The shrub is erect and can attain heights of 2 m. The slender branches are opposite and covered with tiny hairs. The pale-green leaves too are opposite, and elliptical to oval. The flowers are white to pink and broadly funnel-shaped, occurring in clusters at the ends of the twigs. The fruits are waxy, white, berry-like drupes that occur in clusters and often persist through the winter. It is reported that some Indigenous peoples called the berries Ghost Berries or Corpse Berries and would not touch them.

Twinflower

Linnaea borealis

HONEYSUCKLE FAMILY

This small trailing evergreen is common in coniferous forests but easily overlooked by the casual observer. The plant sends runners creeping along the forest floor, over mosses, stumps and fallen logs. At frequent intervals the runners give rise to the distinctive Y-shaped stems 5–10 cm tall. Each fork of the stem supports at its end a pink to white, slightly flared, trumpet-like flower that hangs down like a small lantern on a tiny lamppost. The flowers have a sweet perfume that is most evident near evening.

Death Camas (Meadow Death Camas)

Zigadenus venenosus (also *Toxicoscordion venenosum*)

LILY FAMILY

This plant of moist grasslands, grassy slopes and open woods grows from an onion-like bulb that has no oniony smell. The leaves are mainly basal and resemble grass, with prominent mid-veins. The greenish-white, foul-smelling flowers appear in tight clusters atop an erect stem, each flower having three virtually identical petals and sepals. There are yellowish-green v-shaped glands (nectaries) near the base of the petals and sepals. The plant contains very poisonous alkaloids.

Fairybells

Prosartes hookeri
(form. *Disporum hookeri*)

LILY FAMILY

A plant of moist, shaded woods, stream banks and riverine environments, this delightful flower blooms in early summer. Its creamy-white, bell-shaped flowers have six tepals and occur in drooping pairs at the ends of branches. The leaves of the plant are generally lance-shaped, with parallel veins and pointed ends. The fruits are reddish-orange, egg-shaped berries occurring in pairs. The fruits are edible, but said to be bland. They are a favoured food of many rodents and birds.

False Solomon's Seal

Maianthemum racemosum

LILY FAMILY

A lily of moist woods, rivers and stream banks, thickets and meadows, this plant can grow up to 50 cm tall. The flowers are small and white, arranged in a branching panicle that is upright at the end of the stem. The leaves are broadly lance-shaped, numerous and alternate, gradually tapering to a pointed tip, with prominent parallel veining, sometimes folded at the midline. The fruit is a red berry flecked with maroon.

Prairie Onion

Allium textile

LILY FAMILY

This onion is common in sandy soils in coulees and on dry prairie meadows and hillsides. It is said to be the most abundant of the wild onions. The stems are narrow, grooved and circular, and produce a strong odour of onion if crushed. Several stems can arise from the same bulb. The small, white flowers are numerous and borne in a tight, upright umbel on the top of the stem. This onion usually blooms earlier than other wild onions. Indigenous peoples gathered the bulbs and ate them raw or cooked and in stews and soups.

White Camas

Zigadenus elegans (also *Toxicoscordion elegans*)

LILY FAMILY

This plant of moist grasslands, grassy slopes and open woods grows from an onion-like bulb that has no oniony smell. The greenish-white, foul-smelling flowers appear in open clusters along an erect stem. There are yellowish-green v-shaped glands (nectaries) near the base of the petals and sepals. The leaves are mainly basal and resemble grass, with prominent mid-veins. The species name, *elegans*, means "elegant." Though elegant indeed, these plants are extremely poisonous, containing very toxic alkaloids, particularly in the bulbs.

Other common names include Mountain Death Camas, Green Lily, Elegant Poison Camas, Elegant Death Camas, and Showy Death Camas.

Northern Bedstraw

Galium boreale

MADDER FAMILY

This plant is common to roadsides and woodlands in the montane to subalpine zones. Its tiny white flowers are fragrant and occur in dense clusters at the top of the stems. The individual flowers are cruciform, with each having four spreading petals that are joined at the base. There are no sepals. The smooth stems are square in cross-section and bear whorls of four narrow, lance-shaped leaves, each with three veins. Indigenous peoples used the dried plants to stuff mattresses, and also extracted red and yellow dyes from the plants.

Sweet-Scented Bedstraw

Galium triflorum

MADDER FAMILY

This plant occurs in moist mountain forests, along stream banks and in dense, damp woods. It is a low, trailing perennial that has leaves in whorls of six, radiating from a common centre stem. The leaves are tipped with a sharp point, and give off a sweet aroma, variously compared to vanilla or cinnamon. The small, greenish-white flowers occur in groups of three in the leaf axils, with four petals per flower. Some Indigenous peoples used the plant for stuffing their mattresses.

Seneca Snakeroot

Polygala senega

MILKWORT FAMILY

This multi-stemmed, unbranched, erect perennial grows up to 50 cm tall from a woody, twisted rootstalk that has a snake-like appearance and smells and tastes somewhat like oil of wintergreen. The plant appears in open woods and prairie parklands. Its numerous leaves are alternate, narrowly lance-shaped, simple and up to 30 cm long. The small, numerous flowers are greenish-white and appear in dense, tapered clusters atop the stems. The common name originates from the practice of using the plant to treat snakebite.

Morning Glory (Hedge Bindweed)

Calystegia sepium (also *Convolvulus sepium*)

MORNING GLORY FAMILY

This plant is a twining, climbing or trailing vine that grows from slender, spreading rhizomes. Its white to pinkish flowers are 3–6 cm across and trumpet- or funnel-shaped. The leaves are alternate and arrowhead-shaped, and the flowers appear solitary in the leaf axils. The flowers usually close when it is dark, overcast or raining. Other locally common names for the plant are Lady's Nightcap and Bell-Bind.

Pennycress (Stinkweed)

Thlaspi arvense

MUSTARD FAMILY

This mustard was introduced from Eurasia, and appears at low to mid-elevations in cultivated areas and waste places. It blooms continuously from early spring until frosts arrive. The leaves have irregularly toothed margins and clasp the stalk. The white flowers have four petals and appear in rounded clusters at the tops of the stem. The fruits of the plant are flat, circular pods with wide wings around the edges and a notch at the top. The common name is derived from the resemblance of the fruits to the size of pennies. The common name Stinkweed is appropriate.

Black Henbane

Hyoscyamus niger

NIGHTSHADE FAMILY

These plants are imports from Europe that are looked upon as a noxious weed. The species is biennial and has large, robust, irregularly shaped leaves that grow to about 1 m tall. The flowers are bell-shaped and formed in crowded, one-sided spikes near the top of the plant. The petals have a distinctive and conspicuous network of purple veins, both inside and outside the petals. The flowers mature to a capsule that contains many seeds and resembles a peanut in shape and texture.

Hooded Ladies' Tresses

Spiranthes romanzoffiana

ORCHID FAMILY

This orchid is reasonably common in swampy places, along lakeshores and in meadows and open, shady woods. It grows up to 60 cm tall. The characteristic feature of the plant is its crowded flower spike, which can contain up to 60 densely spaced white flowers that appear to coil around the end of the stem in three spiralling ranks. When newly bloomed, the flower has a wonderful aroma which most people say smells like vanilla. The common name is a reference to the braid-like appearance of the flowers, similar to a braid in a lady's hair.

Round-Leaved Orchid

Amerorchis rotundifolia

ORCHID FAMILY

This tiny orchid, standing no more than 25 cm tall, occurs in well-drained parts of bogs and swamps and in cool, moist, mossy coniferous forests. The flowers are irregular, with three white to pink sepals. The upper sepal combines with the upper two, purple-veined petals to form a hood. The two lateral sepals are wing-like. The lowest petal forms an oblong lip that is white to pink and spotted with dark-red or purple markings. The leaf is basal, solitary and broadly elliptical. These small orchids are always a treat to discover, and in some places they appear in profusion.

Sparrow's-Egg Lady's Slipper (Franklin's Lady's Slipper)

Cypripedium passerinum

ORCHID FAMILY

This lovely orchid grows from a cord-like rhizome along streams and in boggy or mossy coniferous areas. It resembles other Lady's Slippers in shape, but this flower is decidedly smaller, with bright-purple dots on its interior, and has shorter, stubbier, greenish sepals. Both the stem and the leaves of the plant are covered in soft hairs. The species name, *passerinum*, means "sparrow-like," a reference to the spotting on the flower being like the markings on a sparrow egg.

Ground Plum

Astragalus crassicarpus

PEA FAMILY

This hardy perennial grows in open prairie and on grassy hillsides, and sprawls over the ground, sometimes forming dense mats up to 1 m in diameter. The stems are decumbent – lying on the ground, with tips ascending – and the inflorescence appears in a loose raceme of eight to ten pea-like flowers at the tip of the stems. The flowers are whitish, with their keels fringed in purple. The fruits are nearly round pods up to 12 mm in diameter, which are reddish and lie on the ground like small, red plums.

White Clover (Dutch Clover)

Trifolium repens

PEA FAMILY

This common plant was introduced from Eurasia for hay, pasture and soil improvement, it being a nitrogen fixer in the soil. The leaves, which creep along the ground, are composed of three leaflets – occasionally four, if you are lucky. The flowers are white and clustered on short, slender stalks in round heads. On close examination the flower cluster is quite intricate in shape and worthy of close examination. Historically the flowers have been used to flavour cheese and tobacco, and have even been used in famine times to make bread.

White Peavine

Lathyrus ochroleucus

PEA FAMILY

A plant of moist, shaded woods and thicket edges, this twining perennial has coiled tendrils at the ends of its leaves, and it climbs on adjacent plants. Its pea-like flowers are pale yellow to white. *Lathyrus* is from the ancient Greek name for a plant like this or some other member of the pea family. The species name, *ochroleucus*, is Greek, meaning "yellowish white," alluding to the flower colour. The peavines are distinguished from the vetches by their larger leaves and stipules.

Wild Licorice

Glycyrrhiza lepidota

PEA FAMILY

This coarse perennial grows up to 1 m tall from a thick rootstock that has a slight licorice flavour. It occurs in moist grasslands, along streams and rivers and in slough margins and disturbed areas. The leaves are alternate and pinnately compound, with 11–19 pale-green, sharp-pointed, lance-shaped leaflets. The leaflets have glandular dots on the underside, and produce a lemony odour when crushed. The showy, yellowish-white flowers are numerous and occur in dense clusters at the top of the stem.

Moss Phlox

Phlox hoodii

PHLOX FAMILY

This is a plant of dry, exposed hillsides, eroded slopes, foothills and prairies. The small, five petalled flowers with orange stamens are united into a tube below. The tiny, overlapping, grey-green leaves are awl-shaped with spiny tips and woolly at the base. The plant grows low to the ground and covers the ground like a moss. The flowers show a tremendous variance in colour, from white to all shades of blue and purple. The genus name, *Phlox*, is Greek for "flame." This flower blooms early in the spring and adds a wonderful spectrum of colour to an otherwise drab landscape.

Field Chickweed (Mouse-Ear Chickweed)

Cerastium arvense

PINK FAMILY

This early-blooming plant thrives in dry grasslands and rocky and disturbed ground, often forming large mats of white flowers in the spring. The flowers appear in loose clusters, often numerous on each plant. The five white petals are notched and have green lines on them as nectar guides for insects. The upper part of the leaf is said to resemble a mouse's ear, thus the common name for the plant.

Mealy Primrose

Primula incana

PRIMROSE FAMILY

This small plant inhabits moist meadows and slopes and the margins of sloughs and lakes, where it grows low to the ground with a basal rosette of leaves. The flowers are pale purple to white, with yellow centres. The petals are deeply notched and appear at the end of a tubular calyx. The common name refers to the mealy, cream-coloured scales on the undersides of the leaves. *Primula* is from the Latin *primus*, meaning "first," a reference to the early blooming time of many in the genus.

Western Spring Beauty

Claytonia lanceolata

PURSLANE FAMILY

The flowers of this early bloomer are white, but may appear pink, owing to the reddish veins in the petals and the pink anthers. The tips of the petals are distinctly notched. The plants are usually less than 20 cm tall, and the flowers appear in loose, short-stalked terminal clusters. The species grows from a small, white, edible corm. Some Indigenous peoples used the corm as food, and it is said to taste similar to a potato.

Birch-Leaf Spirea

Spiraea betulifolia

ROSE FAMILY

This deciduous shrub grows to 70 cm, and occurs in moist to dry open and wooded sites, from valley floors to the subalpine zone. It spreads by underground runners, and often forms dense cover on the forest floor. The plant is alternately branched, with cinnamon-brown bark and alternate oval or egg-shaped leaves that are irregularly sharp-toothed towards the tip. The flowers are dull white, often tinged to purple or pink, saucer-shaped and occurring in flat-topped clusters on the ends of the stems.

Black Hawthorn

Crataegus douglasii

ROSE FAMILY

This is a large deciduous shrub that can reach up to 8 m in height. The bark is grey, rough and scaly, and the plant has sharp, stout thorns up to 3 cm long that will command immediate attention from the unwary passerby who stumbles into the plant. The leaves are oval-shaped and appear leathery, with multiple lobes at the top. The white, showy flowers are saucer-shaped, occurring in clusters at the tips of the branches. The berries are generally unpalatable dark-purplish pomes that contain a large, hard seed.

Saskatoon (Serviceberry)

Amelanchier alnifolia

ROSE FAMILY

This deciduous shrub grows to heights of up to 5 m or more, and is found in open woods and on stream banks and hillsides, from the prairie to montane elevations. The shrub is erect to spreading, with smooth bark that is reddish when new, turning greyish with age. The leaves are alternate, oval to round in shape, rounded at the tips and sharp-toothed on the upper half. The white flowers are star-shaped, with five slender petals about 2 cm across, and occur in clusters near the branch tips. The purple fruits are sweet and juicy, berry-like pomes.

Trailing Raspberry
Rubus pubescens

ROSE FAMILY

This dwarf shrub is a low, trailing plant with slender runners and erect flowering stems that grows at low to mid-elevations in moist to wet forests and clearings. The plant has soft hairs on it, but no prickles. The leaves are palmately divided into three oval or diamond-shaped leaflets, with pointed tips and toothed margins. The flowers are white and spreading, and occur on short, erect branches. The fruits are red drupelets, and the aggregate cluster makes up a raspberry. The fruits are also referred to as Dewberries.

White Cinquefoil
Potentilla arguta

ROSE FAMILY

This species grows tall – up to 1 m – in grasslands and meadows. It is a glandular hairy plant, and bears creamy white flowers with yellow centres in a compact arrangement. Its leaves are bright green and pinnately compound. The basal leaves have 7–11 toothed, hairy leaflets, while the upper leaves have three to five leaflets. The genus name, *Potentilla*, is derived from the Latin *potens*, meaning "powerful," most probably a reference to the potent medicinal properties of some of the herbs in the genus. Potentillas have a high tannin content, making them astringent and anti-inflammatory.

Wild Strawberry

Fragaria virginiana

ROSE FAMILY

This is a plant of shaded to open gravelly soils and thickets, from prairie to alpine habitats. The single five-petalled white flower appears on a leafless stem that is usually shorter than the leaves are long. The stamens are numerous and yellow. The leaves are rounded to broadly oval and toothed, with three leaflets on short stalks. The fruit is a red berry covered with sunken, seed-like achenes. New plants are often established from reddish runners. Strawberry is said to come from the Anglo-Saxon name *streowberie* because the runners from the plant are strewn across the ground.

Pale Comandra (Bastard Toadflax)

Comandra umbellata

SANDALWOOD FAMILY

This erect, blue-green perennial springs from a creeping rootstock, and is common in open pine woods, and grasslands and on gravel slopes. Its leaves are lance-shaped and hug the erect stem. The flowers occur in a rounded or flat-topped cluster atop the stem. Each flower is greenish-white, with the sepals separated above and fused into a small funnel below. The plant has another common name – Bastard Toadflax – though the plant bears no relationship to Toadflax and is not in any way similar. Pale Comandra is a parasite, taking water, and perhaps food, from its host plant.

Richardson's Alumroot

Heuchera richardsonii

SAXIFRAGE FAMILY

This is an erect perennial that grows up to 40 cm tall in sandy, gravelly grasslands, on rocky slopes and along streams. Its leathery, long-stemmed leaves are all basal, round to heart-shaped, lobed and sharp-toothed. The numerous flowers are glandular hairy, cream to pinkish and appear in a spiral around the top of a tall, leafless flower stalk. The common name, Alumroot, is a reference to the alum-like astringent found in the root of the plant. Indigenous peoples used the plant medicinally for a variety of ailments.

Western Canada Violet

Viola canadensis

VIOLET FAMILY

This plant favours moist to fairly dry deciduous forests, floodplains and clearings. The flowers are held on aerial stems, and are white with yellow bases. The lower three petals have purple lines, the upper two a purplish tinge on the back. The leaves are heart-shaped, long-stalked and decidedly pointed at the tip, with saw-toothed edges. This small white flower splashes shady woods and marshes in midsummer. The plant grows from short, thick rhizomes with slender, creeping runners. These violets are easily propagated from runners but can be invasive in a garden setting.

Blue *and* **Purple Flowers**

This section includes flowers that are predominantly blue or purple when encountered in the field, ranging from pale blue to deep purple and from light violet to lavender. Some of the lighter hues of blue and purple might shade into pinks, so if you do not find the flower you are looking for here, check the other parts of the book.

Common Butterwort
Pinguicula vulgaris

BLADDERWORT FAMILY

This small plant is one of only a few carnivorous ones in the region. It grows from fibrous roots in bogs, seeps and wetlands and along stream banks and lakeshores from valleys to the subalpine zone. Its pale-green to yellowish leaves are basal, short-stalked, somewhat overlapping and curled in at the margins, forming a rosette on the ground. The leaves have glandular hairs on their upper surface which exude a sticky substance that attracts and then ensnares small insects. The flower is pale to dark purple and solitary atop a leafless stem.

Stickseed
Hackelia floribunda

BORAGE FAMILY

This hairy biennial or short-lived perennial has stiffly erect stems and grows to 1 m tall. The small, yellow-centred blue flowers occur in loose clusters on curving stalks near the top of the plant. The fruits are nutlets that are keeled in the middle and attached to a pyramid-shaped base. Each nutlet has rows of barbed prickles. While the flowers on this plant are lovely to look at, the prickles on the nutlets cling easily to fur, feathers and clothing, thus lending the plant its common name.

Tall Lungwort (Mertensia)

Mertensia paniculata

BORAGE FAMILY

This perennial grows from a woody rootstock to heights of some 80 cm along stream banks and in moist woods, shaded poplar groves and mixed forests. The plant is usually hairy and may have multiple branches. Its basal leaves are large, prominently veined, heart-shaped, white-hairy on both sides and long-stalked. The stem leaves are stalkless or short-stalked, rounded at the base and tapering to the pointed tip. The blue flowers occur in drooping clusters, hanging like small bells. The corolla is tubular and five-lobed. The flowers' buds often have a pinkish tinge, turning blue as they open.

Blue Clematis

Clematis occidentalis

BUTTERCUP FAMILY

A plant of shaded riverine woods and thickets, Clematis is a climbing, slightly hairy, reddish-stemmed vine that attaches itself to other plants by slender tendrils. The flowers have four to five sepals and are purplish to blue in colour, with dark veins. The flowers resemble crepe paper. The fruits are mop-like clusters of seeds, each of which has a long feathery style. The Blackfoot called the plant "ghost's lariat," a reference to the fact that the vine would entangle their feet when they walked through it. Clematis often goes by the locally common name of Virgin's Bower.

Blue Columbine
Aquilegia brevistyla

BUTTERCUP FAMILY

This plant occurs in deciduous, coniferous and mixed woods, meadows and riverine environments, and grows to heights of 80 cm. The leaves are mostly basal and compound, with each having three sets of three leaflets. The flowers appear on tall stems that reach above the basal leaves. The flowering stems have a small number of smaller leaves, each with only three leaflets. The attractive flowers can be nodding or ascending, with five yellowish or white sepals and five blue to purplish reflexed petals, each with a hooked, nectar-producing spur at its end. Columbines have a very distinctive floral structure and are usually unmistakable. Bumblebees and butterflies are drawn to them to collect the nectar.

Low Larkspur
Delphinium bicolor

BUTTERCUP FAMILY

This is a plant of open woods, grasslands and slopes that grows up to 40 cm tall from a fleshy rootstock. It usually has a single flowering stem. Larkspurs are easily recognized for their showy, highly modified flowers. The irregular petals are whitish to bluish, with sepals that are blue to violet. The upper sepal forms a large, hollow, nectar-producing spur. The flowers bloom up the stem in a loose, elongated cluster. The common name is said to have originated because the spur on the flower resembles the spur on the foot of a lark. The plant is poisonous to cattle and humans.

Prairie Crocus

Anemone patens
(also *Pulsatilla patens*)

BUTTERCUP FAMILY

This plant is widespread and common in grasslands, dry meadows and mountain slopes. It is usually one of the first wildflowers to bloom in the spring, and can occur in huge numbers. The flowers are usually solitary, various blues to purples in colour, and cup-shaped. White varieties are sometimes seen. It is interesting to note that the flower blooms before the basal leaves appear. The plant has many basal leaves, palmately divided into three main leaflets, and again divided into narrow linear segments. The leaves on the flower stem appear in a whorl of three.

Blue Lettuce

Lactuca tatarica
ssp. *pulchella*

COMPOSITE FAMILY

This plant grows up to 1 m tall in fields and meadows and along roadsides, lakeshores and stream banks, often in moist, heavy soil. The leaves are hairless, lobed below and simple above. The flowers are composite heads and have pale to dark-blue ray florets that are toothed at the tip. There are no disc florets.

Bull Thistle

Cirsium vulgare

COMPOSITE FAMILY

This Eurasian weed was introduced to North America and is now common along roadsides and in pastures, waste places and clearings. The flowers are large composite heads with purple disc flowers and no ray flowers. The flower heads are bulbous and covered in sharp spikes. The flower structure is extraordinarily intricate when examined closely. The leaves, both basal and stem, are lance shaped, deeply lobed, spiny and clasping the stem. The species grows to heights of over 2 m and produces a multitude of flowers, which are a favourite of bees and butterflies.

Canada Thistle

Cirsium arvense

COMPOSITE FAMILY

Despite the common name, this noxious weed was introduced to North America from Eurasia. The plant grows to over 1 m tall from a thin, white creeping rhizome. The flowers occur in heads at the tops of the multiple branches. The flowers are usually pinkish to mauve but may be white. The leaves are alternate and oblong to lance-shaped with wavy margins. Because of the creeping rhizome and tremendous seed distribution, the plant will quickly take over areas where it grows. If the rhizome is cut or broken by farming machinery, the spread of the plant is exacerbated.

Parry's Townsendia

Townsendia parryi

COMPOSITE FAMILY

This tap-rooted, reddish-stemmed perennial blooms in the early spring on dry hills and gravelly slopes, along stream banks and in grassy areas from prairie to alpine elevations. Most of its leaves are basal and form a rosette at ground level. The stems, leaves and bracts are covered in white hairs. The relatively large flowers appear low to the ground on short stems, and they consist of broad ray flowers of violet to purple surrounding bright-yellow disc flowers. The Blackfoot boiled the roots of some Townsendias to make a concoction for treating ailments in horses.

Showy Aster

Aster conspicuus

COMPOSITE FAMILY

This plant is widespread and common at low to mid-elevations in moist to dry open forests, openings, clearings and meadows. The flowers are few to many composite heads on glandular stalks, with 15–35 violet ray flowers and yellow disc flowers. The stem leaves are egg-shaped to elliptical, with sharp-toothed edges and clasping bases. Some Indigenous peoples soaked the roots of the plant in water and used the decoction to treat boils. The leaves were also used as a poultice for that purpose.

Smooth Blue Aster

Aster laevis

COMPOSITE FAMILY

This plant inhabits open wooded areas, meadows, coulees and ditches, often on gravelly soil. The plants are erect, up to 120 cm tall, and can form large colonies. The flowers are composed of pale- to dark-purple or bluish ray florets surrounding bright-yellow disc florets. Smooth Blue Aster is believed to be a selenium absorber and therefore dangerous to livestock that consume it. Selenium is a chemical element that is accumulative in the digestive system, and too much can lead to symptoms like the blind staggers.

Small-Flowered Beardtongue (Slender Beardtongue)

Penstemon procerus

FIGWORT FAMILY

This plant grows up to 40 cm tall at low to alpine elevations, usually in dry to moist open forests, grassy clearings, meadows and disturbed areas. Most of the blunt to lance-shaped leaves appear in opposite pairs up the stem. The small blue to purple flowers are funnel-shaped and appear in one to several tight clusters arranged in whorls around the stem and at its tip.

Smooth Blue Beardtongue

Penstemon nitidus

FIGWORT FAMILY

This erect, often branched perennial usually has several stems that grow to 30 cm tall, often occurring in clumps on dry, grassy slopes and in eroded areas. The pale-green, oval to lance-shaped leaves are opposite, thick and fleshy and covered with a greyish bloom. The blue flowers are numerous, and occur in dense clusters from the leaf axils at the top of the plant. The flowers are tube-shaped, up to 2 cm long, and have purple pencilling inside the lower floral lip.

Blue Flax

Linum lewisii

FLAX FAMILY

This perennial grows up to 60 cm tall from a woody base and taproot, in grasslands, along roadsides and on dry, exposed hillsides and gravelly river flats. The leaves are alternate, simple and stalkless. The pale purplish-blue flowers have five petals, five sepals, five styles and five stamens, with darkish guidelines, and are yellowish at the base. They appear on very slender stems that are constantly moving, even with the smallest of breezes. Some Indigenous peoples used the stem fibres to make cordage. The common name, Flax, is derived from the Latin *filum*, which means "thread."

Hairy Four O'Clock (Umbrellawort)

Mirabilis hirsuta

FOUR O'CLOCK FAMILY

This perennial grows from a heavy, woody taproot in pastures, reaching 60 cm in height. The plant is covered in short hairs. The leaves are opposite, variable in shape, and up to 10 cm long. The flowers are bluish to pinkish, and often occur in groups of three on the upper half of the plant. The common name Four O'Clock comes from the fact that many members of the genus have flowers that open in the late afternoon. The species name, *hirsuta*, is derived from Latin and means "hairy." Plants in the genus are often referred to as Umbrellaworts.

Northern Gentian

Gentianella amarella
(also *Gentiana amarella*)

GENTIAN FAMILY

This plant is found in moist places in meadows, woods and ditches and along stream banks up to the subalpine zone. The flowers are first sighted by their star-like formation winking at the top of the corolla tube, amidst adjacent grasses. The plant is most often small, standing only 15–20 cm. The flowers appear in clusters in the axils of the upper stem leaves, the leaves being opposite and appearing almost to be small hands holding up the flowers for inspection. There is a fringe inside the throat of the flower.

Sticky Purple Geranium

Geranium viscosissimum

GERANIUM FAMILY

This is a plant of moist grasslands, open woods and thickets that can grow up to 60 cm tall. The flowers have large, showy, rose-purple to bluish petals that are strongly veined with purple. The long-stalked leaves are deeply lobed and split into five to seven sharp-toothed divisions, appearing in opposite pairs along the stem. There are sticky, glandular hairs covering the stems, leaves and some flower parts. The fruit is an elongated, glandular hairy capsule with a long beak shaped like a stork's or crane's bill. The specific epithet, *viscosissimum*, derives from Latin and is the superlative form of "sticky."

Harebell

Campanula rotundifolia

HAREBELL FAMILY

This plant is widespread in a variety of habitats, including grasslands, gullies, moist forests, clearings and rocky open ground. The bell-shaped flowers are purplish-blue, with hairless sepals, nodding on a thin stem in loose clusters. The leaves are lance-shaped and thin on the stem. The heart-shaped basal leaves are coarse-toothed and usually wither before the flowers appear. *Campanula* is Latin meaning "little bell."

Western Bog Laurel (Swamp Laurel)

Kalmia microphylla

HEATH FAMILY

This low-growing evergreen shrub occurs in cool bogs and along stream banks and lakeshores from low to subalpine elevations. Its leathery leaves are dark green above and greyish white beneath, often with the margins rolled under. The flowers are pink to rose coloured, with the petals fused together to form a saucer or bowl on a reddish stalk. There are 10 purple-tipped stamens protruding from the petals. The leaves and flowers of this plant contain poisonous alkaloids that can be fatal to humans and livestock if ingested.

Blue-Eyed Grass

Sisyrinchium angustifolium

IRIS FAMILY

These beautiful flowers can be found scattered among the grasses of moist meadows from low to sub-alpine elevations. The distinctively flattened stems grow to 30 cm and are twice as tall as the grass-like basal leaves. The blue flower is star-shaped, with three virtually identi-cal petals and sepals, each tipped with a minute point. There is a bright-yellow eye in the centre of the flower. The blossoms are very short-lived, wilting usually within a day, to be replaced by fresh ones on the succeeding day.

Giant Hyssop

Agastache foeniculum

MINT FAMILY

A plant common in thickets and along streams, this mint is erect and grows to heights of up to 1 m. The stem is square in cross-sec-tion, typical of the mint family. The leaves are opposite, oval and coarse-toothed, with pointed tips. The blue to purple flowers are densely packed and appear in in-terrupted clusters along the top of the stem. Indigenous peoples used the leaves of the plant for making a tea and as a flavouring in foods. The flowers were often collected for medicine bundles.

Marsh Hedge Nettle

Stachys palustris

MINT FAMILY

A plant of wetland margins, stream banks, marshes and wet ditches, Marsh Hedge Nettle grows erect to heights of up to 40 cm. The stems are square, the leaves opposite and simple, lance-shaped and hairy. The flowers are pale purple and appear at the top of the spike, often in interrupted fashion.

The genus name, *Stachys*, is Greek for "spike," referring to the inflorescence type. The specific epithet, *palustris*, is Latin meaning "of wet places."

Marsh Skullcap

Scutellaria galericulata

MINT FAMILY

This plant grows up to 80 cm tall at low to mid-elevations in wetlands and ditches and along lakeshores and stream banks. Its leaves are opposite, oval to lance-shaped, and irregularly scalloped along the blades. The stem is square, typical of the mint family. The trumpet-shaped flowers have a hooded upper lip and a broad, hairless lower lip, and are blue to purplish-pink marked with white. The flowers occur as solitary on slender stalks or as pairs in the leaf axils.

Wild Mint (Field Mint)

Mentha arvensis

MINT FAMILY

This plant inhabits wetland marshes, moist woods, stream banks and lake shores, and sometimes lives in shallow water. The purplish to pinkish to bluish flowers are crowded in dense clusters in the upper leaf axils. The leaves are opposite, prominently veined, and highly scented of mint if crushed. The stems are square in cross section and hairy. The strong, distinctive taste of mint is from their volatile oils. The leaves have long been used fresh, dried or frozen as a flavouring and for teas.

Dame's Rocket (Dame's Violet)

Hesperis matronalis

MUSTARD FAMILY

This mustard was introduced into North America from Eurasia as an ornamental plant, and it has spread extensively throughout Canada and much of the United States. Typically it inhabits disturbed sites, waste ground, thickets, woods and road and railsides. The plant is erect and grows to over 1 m tall. Its lance-shaped leaves are alternate, predominantly clasping on the stem, hairy on both sides, and become progressively smaller up the stem. The flowers occur in showy clusters at the top of the stem. Each flower is four-petalled, purple to blue to white in colour, and fragrant.

Venus Slipper (Fairy Slipper)

Calypso bulbosa

ORCHID FAMILY

This orchid is found in moist, shaded coniferous forests. The flowers are solitary and nodding on leafless stems. The flower has pinkish to purplish sepals and mauve side petals. The lip is whitish or purplish with red to purple spots or stripes and is hairy yellow inside. The flower is on the top of a single stalk and has a deeply wrinkled appearance. This small but extraordinarily beautiful flower blooms in the early spring, often occurring in colonies.

Ascending Purple Milk Vetch

Astragalus adsurgens

PEA FAMILY

This tufted, erect or spreading perennial grows up to 50 cm tall from a heavy taproot in grasslands and meadows. The leaves are pinnately compound, greyish-green in colour and hairy. Each leaf may contain 9–25 leaflets. The plant usually has a dozen or more stems, and forms clumps up to 60 cm wide. The flowers occur in dense rounded or cylindrical clusters, and may be white, purplish or lavender. The standard usually has dark markings, and the keel is dark-tinged.

The plant is also known as Standing Milk Vetch and Lavender Milk Vetch.

Purple Milk Vetch

Astragalus agrestis

PEA FAMILY

This plant occurs in grasslands and meadows from prairie to subalpine elevations. It is a low-growing, hairy plant that may be erect or decumbent. The leaves are compound, with 9–23 spear-shaped leaflets that are often notched on their blunt ends. The flowers are purple to pink, and occur in densely packed, rounded clusters which are enclosed by a calyx that has greyish to blackish hairs.

Purple Prairie Clover

Petalostemon purpureum

PEA FAMILY

This perennial is a many-stemmed, decumbent or erect, smooth, leafy plant that grows up to 60 cm tall from a thick rootstock. It occurs on hillsides, in open prairie, at roadsides and on eroded slopes in badlands. The leaves are medium green, alternate and pinnately compound. The small flowers are numerous, dark-purple to rose in colour, and each has five petals of almost the same size and shape, but without the keel that is typical of pea flowers. The flowers are most often seen at the base of the spike, with a bare area above, similar to coneflowers.

Showy Locoweed
Oxytropis splendens

PEA FAMILY

This attractive member of the pea family has silvery leaves growing from a branched, woody stock. The flower stalk is elongated and holds dense clusters of numerous flowers above the silvery leaves. The flowers are purple to bluish and shaped like other members of the pea family. Locoweeds are poisonous to cattle, horses and sheep because the plants contain an alkaloid that can cause the blind staggers, a condition that makes the animal behave in a crazy fashion, ergo *loco* in Spanish.

Silky Lupine
Lupinus sericeus

PEA FAMILY

This leafy, erect, tufted perennial with stout stems appears in sandy to gravelly grasslands, open woods, and roadsides, often growing in dense clumps or bunches. The plant grows up to 80 cm tall. Its flowers are showy in long, dense terminal clusters, and display a variety of colours in blues and purples, occasionally white and yellow. The flowers have a typical pea shape, with a strongly truncated keel and a pointed tip. The leaves of Lupines are very distinctive, being palmately compound and alternate on the stem, with five to nine very narrow leaflets that have silky hairs on both sides.

Shooting Star

Dodecatheon pulchellum

PRIMROSE FAMILY

This plant is scattered and locally common at low to alpine elevations in warm, dry climates, mountain meadows, grasslands and stream banks. The leaves are lance- to spatula-shaped and appear in a basal rosette. The singular to several purple to lavender flowers nod atop a leafless stalk, with corolla lobes turned backwards. The stamens are united into a yellow to orange tube from which the style and anthers protrude. A harbinger of spring, these lovely flowers often bloom in huge numbers, turning the grasslands to a purple hue.

Bog Violet

Viola nephrophylla

VIOLET FAMILY

This beautiful small violet grows in moist meadows, on stream banks and in woods. The leaves and flower stalks arise from the base of the plant. The leaves are oval to kidney-shaped, smooth, and scalloped on the margins. The purple to blue flowers each have a spur 2–3 mm long. Violets are high in vitamins C and A and have been used as food since early Greek and Roman times. They are still cultivated for that purpose in some parts of Europe. The young leaves and flower buds may be used in salads or boiled.

Yellow Flowers

This section includes flowers that are predominantly yellow when encountered in the field. Their colours vary from bright yellow to pale cream. Some of the species listed here have other colour variations, so you might have to check other parts of the book to find the one you're looking for. For example, the Paintbrushes (*Castilleja* spp.) have a yellow variation but they are most often encountered as red, so they are pictured in that section for purposes of sorting.

Common Bladderwort

Utricularia vulgaris

BLADDERWORT FAMILY

This aquatic carnivorous plant is found in shallow water in sloughs, lakes, ditches and ponds. It floats beneath the surface of the water, with a tangle of coarse stems and leaves. The long, branching, submerged stems have finely divided leaves that spread out like little nets. Attached to the leaves hang numerous small bladders that are actually traps for aquatic insects. When an insect swims into a bladder, small hairs are tripped, which shuts the bladder, trapping the insect inside. The insects are then digested, providing a source of nitrogen for the plant.

Puccoon (Lemonweed)

Lithospermum ruderale

BORAGE FAMILY

A coarse perennial up to 50 cm tall, this plant is firmly anchored to dry slopes and grasslands by a large woody taproot. The numerous sharp-pointed leaves are lance-shaped and clasp the stem. The small yellow flowers are partly hidden in the axils of the leaves near the top of the plant, and have a strong, pleasant scent. The stems and leaves are covered in long white hairs. The fruit is an oval, cream-coloured nutlet that is somewhat pitted and resembles pointed teeth.

Western False Gromwell

Onosmodium molle

BORAGE FAMILY

A leafy perennial that grows up to 80 cm tall, this plant is found on gravel banks and dry slopes and in dry woods in the southern part of the region. The leaves are numerous, sessile (stalkless), lance-shaped, prominently veined and very hairy. The flowers are yellowish-white and occur in crowded clusters in the top third of the stem. Long styles protrude from the flowers. The fruits are hard, pearly-white nutlets. The common name Western False Gromwell arises because this plant is thought to resemble Puccoons, which are often referred to as Gromwells.

Clustered Broomrape

Orobanche fasciculata

BROOMRAPE FAMILY

This plant is a relatively rare parasitic perennial that grows to heights of 15 cm in grasslands and dry open forests, often using sagebrushes as host plants. The "leaves" on the plant are brownish scales. The flower stalks are fleshy, glandular hairy, brown and often yellowish or purple-tinged. Three to ten flowers appear atop the stalks. The flowers have a purplish or yellowish, tube-shaped corolla with two lips, the upper lip being two-lobed, the lower, three. These plants get their nutrients from the host plant.

Yellow Buckwheat (Umbrella Plant)

Eriogonum flavum

BUCKWHEAT FAMILY

This fuzzy-haired, tufted perennial favours dry, often sandy or rocky outcrops, eroded slopes and badlands. The leaves are dark green on top, but appear white to felty on the underside due to the dense hairs. The yellow flowers occur in compound umbels – umbrella-shaped clusters – atop the stem. The common name, Umbrella Plant, is testimony to the shape of the inflorescence.

Creeping Buttercup (Seaside Buttercup)

Ranunculus cymbalaria

BUTTERCUP FAMILY

This plant spreads over the ground by slender, creeping stems or runners, similar to those of the Wild Strawberry. Its long-stalked leaf blades are egg- or heart-shaped and have scalloped margins. The plant is found in moist meadows, on stream banks and at the margins of lakes and ponds. Buttercups are among the oldest of flower families, having existed for millions of years, and are considered one of the most primitive plant families. The cell structure of the petals is such that there is air in the cell vacuoles, and this is responsible for the "whiteness" seen on the petals.

Marsh Marigold

Caltha palustris

BUTTERCUP FAMILY

Favouring wet meadows, woods and bogs, this plant is often found in shallow water of slow-moving streams and ditches. The flower has five to nine bright-yellow, showy sepals, but no petals. Its large leaves are mostly basal and quite distinctive, being dark green and round to kidney- or heart-shaped. The common name is said to have come from Mary's Gold, a reference to a yellow flower esteemed by the Virgin Mary. All parts of the mature plant are poisonous, but they are said to be distasteful to livestock because of the acrid juice.

Meadow Buttercup

Ranunculus acris

BUTTERCUP FAMILY

Among the tallest of the Butter-cups, this plant may reach almost 1 m in height. It is a hairy peren-nial, with broad leaves that are deeply lobed and divided nearly to the base. The flowers are glossy yellow, with greenish hairy sepals that fall off soon after the flower blooms. The species name, *acris*, means "acrid," referring to the juice of this plant. All of the Buttercups contain poisonous compounds.

Prickly-Pear Cactus

Opuntia polyacantha

CACTUS FAMILY

This easily recognized plant is pros-trate and can form mats on dry, ex-posed slopes in eroded areas and badlands, often growing on sandy or rocky soil. The stems are flat-tened and covered with clusters of hard, sharp spines that have tufts of sharp bristles at the base. The flowers are large and showy, with numerous yellow petals that are waxy and up to 5 cm long. There is a large, con-spicuous green stigma and numerous yellow or orange stamens inside the flower. The reddish fruits are soft, spiny berries which are edible and often browsed by antelope.

Heart-Leaved Alexanders (Meadow Parsnip)

Zizia aptera

CARROT FAMILY

This is a plant of prairies, moist meadows, open woods, stream banks and wetland margins. Its small, bright-yellow flowers are numerous and occur in compound, flat-topped clusters at the top of the stems. The lower leaves are leathery, dark green and heart-shaped. The stem leaves are smaller and divided into three leaflets. The stem leaves become progressively smaller along the stem until they become cleft leaflets. The flowers appear on top of hollow stems that are erect and reach heights of up to 60 cm.

Leafy Musineon

Musineon divaricatum

CARROT FAMILY

This plant is a spreading or erect low-growing perennial that can reach 20 cm tall from a thick, swollen taproot. It occurs in dry grasslands and on slopes with southerly or westerly exposures. The leaves are bright green and resemble parsley leaves, with many dissected leaflets. The flowers are yellow, with five rounded petals, and occur in compact umbels atop the rough, glandular flower stalk. A number of such umbels can be found on each plant.

Snakeroot

Sanicula marilandica

CARROT FAMILY

This erect perennial grows up to 1 m tall from thick rootstock in moist woods, shady aspen groves and damp areas near waterways. The basal leaves are long-stalked and palmately divided into five to seven leaflets. The leaves are generally lance-shaped, with sharp-toothed edges. The stem leaves are short-stalked or stalkless. The flowers appear in round clusters and can be yellow-ish, greenish-white or white. The common name, Snakeroot, arises from a practice by Indigenous peoples of using the plant in poultices to treat snakebite.

Arrow-Leaved Balsamroot

Balsomorhiza sagittata

COMPOSITE FAMILY

This is a widespread and frequently abundant plant of hot, arid climates, often found on rocky, south-facing slopes. Its flowers are solitary composite heads with bright-yellow ray flowers and yellow disc flowers, and are densely hairy, especially at the base. The large, silvery leaves are arrowhead-shaped and covered with dense, felt-like hairs. Balsamroot often provides a showy early-spring splash of colour on warm, dry hillsides. All parts of the plant are edible, and the species was an important food for Indigenous peoples.

Black-Eyed Susan

Rudbeckia hirta

COMPOSITE FAMILY

This introduced biennial or short-lived perennial grows up to 1 m tall in meadows and disturbed areas and along roadsides. The plant is rough hairy throughout, and has purplish or reddish simple to branched stems. The leaves are alternate and hairy. The lower leaves are elliptical, sometimes slightly toothed, and long-stalked. The upper leaves are narrow, lance-shaped and short-stalked or sessile. The flower heads appear at the top of long stalks, and consist of 8–20 bright-yellow to orange ray florets surrounding a cone of dark-purple to brown disc florets.

Brown-Eyed Susan

Gaillardia aristata

COMPOSITE FAMILY

This is a plant of open grasslands, dry hillsides, roadsides and open woods. The flowers are large and showy, with yellow ray florets that are purplish to reddish at the base. The central disc is purplish and woolly hairy. The leaves are numerous, alternate and lance-shaped, usually looking greyish and rough owing to the many short hairs. A number of Indigenous peoples used the plant to relieve a variety of ailments.

Colorado Rubber Weed

Hymenoxys richardsonii

COMPOSITE FAMILY

This perennial grows up to 30 cm tall from a woody rootstock, and occurs on dry, rocky or eroded slopes, in grasslands and badlands and along roadsides. The leaves are mostly basal, and all are divided into narrow, smooth, rubbery segments. The flowers have a few yellow ray florets, three-lobed at their tips, and yellow disc florets. The flower heads are borne at the ends of branches in flat-topped clusters. The chief difference between this plant and the related Stemless Rubber Weed is in the leaves.

Prairie Coneflower

Ratibida columnifera

COMPOSITE FAMILY

This is a plant of dry grasslands, coulees and disturbed areas that can reach heights of up to 60 cm. Its greyish-green leaves are alternate and deeply divided into oblong lobes. The distinctive flower appears atop a tall, slender stem, and consists of dark-purple disc florets formed into a cylinder up to 4 cm long, the base of which is surrounded by bright-yellow ray florets. The origin of the genus name, *Ratibida*, is unknown. The species name, *columnifera*, is a reference to the column or cone-shaped inflorescence.

Stemless Rubber Weed (Butte Marigold)

Hymenoxys acaulis

COMPOSITE FAMILY

This creeping, tufted, hairy perennial grows up to 30 cm tall from a woody rootstock, and often forms small colonies. It occurs on dry, rocky or sandy exposed slopes, in grasslands and badlands and along roadsides. The softly hairy leaves are all basal, entire and narrowly lance- to spoon-shaped. The flowers are bright-yellow solitary heads borne on leafless stalks. The yellow ray flowers are three-lobed at the tip, and they reflex with age. The disc flowers are yellow or orange-yellow.

Yellow Evening Primrose

Oenothera villosa
(also *O. strigosa*)

EVENING PRIMROSE FAMILY

An erect, robust, leafy biennial, this plant forms a rosette of leaves the first year, and puts up a tall, leafy stem the second. The flowers have large, bright-yellow, cross-shaped stigma with numerous yellow stamens. The flowers usually open in the evening and fade in the morning, a behaviour adopted because moths are the principal pollinators of the plant. The plant gets its common name by its habit of blooming at dusk.

Yellow Beardtongue (Yellow Penstemon)

Penstemon confertus

FIGWORT FAMILY

This is a plant of moist to dry meadows, woodlands, stream banks, hillsides and mountains. Its small, pale-yellow flowers are numerous and appear in whorled, interrupted clusters along the upper part of the stem. Each flower is tube-shaped and has two lips. The lower lip is three-lobed and bearded at the throat, while the upper one is two-lobed. The common name, Beardtongue, describes the hairy, tongue-like staminode (sterile stamen) in the throat of the flower. The genus name, *Penstemon*, is a reference to the five stamens in the flower.

Yellow Monkeyflower

Mimulus guttatus

FIGWORT FAMILY

This plant occurs, often in large patches, along streams, at seeps and in moist meadows. The species is quite variable, but is always spectacular when found. The bright-yellow flowers resemble Snapdragons, and occur in clusters. They usually have red or purple dots on the lip, giving the appearance of a grinning face. The genus name, *Mimulus*, is derived from the Latin *mimus*, meaning "mimic" or "actor."

Golden Corydalis

Corydalis aurea

FUMITORY FAMILY

This plant of open woods, road-sides, disturbed places and stream banks is an erect or spreading, branched, leafy biennial or annual. It germinates in the fall and over-winters as a seedling. In the spring, it grows rapidly, flowers, and then dies. The yellow flowers are irregu-larly shaped, rather like the flowers of the pea family, with keels at the tips. A long, nectar-producing spur extends backward from the upper petal.

Twining Honeysuckle

Lonicera dioica

HONEYSUCKLE FAMILY

This plant is a flowering vine that clambers over low bushes and shrubs and around tree trunks at low elevations. The trum-pet-shaped flowers cluster inside a shallow cup formed by two leaves that are joined at their bases. The cupped leaves are very distinct-ive and are referred to as "connate" leaves. When the flowers first appear they are yellow, turning orange to brick col-our with age. The five petals are united into a funnel-shaped tube which has a swollen knob near the base where nectar accumulates.

Yellowbell
Fritillaria pudica

LILY FAMILY

This diminutive flower is a harbinger of spring, often blooming just after snowmelt in dry grasslands and dry, open ponderosa pine forests. It can easily be overlooked because of its small size, usually standing only about 15 cm tall. The yellow, drooping, bell-shaped flowers are very distinctive. The flowers turn orange to brick-red as they age. The leaves, usually two or three, are linear to lance-shaped, and appear more or less opposite about halfway up the stem. The Yellowbell sometimes appears with two flowers on a stem, but single blooms are more common.

Prairie Rocket
Erysimum asperum

MUSTARD FAMILY

This erect, robust plant grows up to 50 cm tall or more in dry, sandy grasslands, particularly in the southeastern parts of the region. The bright-yellow flowers grow at the terminal ends of stout branching stems, and appear in rounded clusters. The stem leaves on the plant are simple, alternate and lance-shaped. At one time, children were treated for worms with a concoction made from the crushed seeds of this plant mixed in water.

Soopolallie (Canadian Buffaloberry)

Shepherdia canadensis

OLEASTER FAMILY

This deciduous shrub grows up to 3 m tall, and is often the dominant understorey in lodgepole pine forests. All parts of the plant are covered with shiny, rust-coloured scales, giving the whole plant an orange, rusty appearance. The leaves are leathery and thick, green and glossy on the upper surface, while the lower surface is covered with white hairs and sprinkled with rust-coloured dots. The male and female flowers appear on separate plants. The small, inconspicuous yellow flowers often appear on the branches of the plant prior to the arrival of the leaves.

Wolf Willow (Silverberry)

Elaeagnus commutata

OLEASTER FAMILY

This deciduous shrub grows up to 4 m tall, often in dense stands. Its twigs are thickly covered with rusty-brown scales, while its oval, silvery leaves are alternate and similarly covered with small scales. The flowers are funnel-shaped and have four yellow lobes, occurring at the leaf axils. The flowers are very fragrant with a distinctive aroma. The fruits are silvery, round to egg-shaped berries, and usually persist throughout the winter.

Yellow Lady's Slipper
Cypripedium parviflorum

ORCHID FAMILY

This is an orchid of bogs, damp woods and stream banks. Its broadly elliptical leaves are clasping and alternate, with two to four per stem. The yellow flowers usually occur as a single on a stem, and resemble a small shoe. The sepals and lateral petals are similar, greenish-yellow to brownish, with twisted, wavy margins. The lower petal forms a prominent pouch-shaped yellow lip with purple dotting around the puckered opening. This flower has suffered large range reductions as a result of picking and attempted transplantation, which almost always fails.

Buffalo Bean (Golden Bean)
Thermopsis rhombifolia

PEA FAMILY

This plant occurs on grassy hillsides, roadsides, ditches and prairies, often forming large clumps. The flower is bright yellow and blooms in crowded clusters atop the stem, which grows to 35 cm tall. The flower has the typical pea shape, with the keel enclosing the stamens. The leaves are opposite, alternate, compound and clasping leaflets. The plant takes its common name from Blackfoot parlance. The Blackfoot took the flower's blooming as a sign to go hunting buffalo, the buffalo having fattened on spring grasses. Buffalo did not eat these flowers, though, because the plant contains poisonous alkaloids.

Caragana
Caragana arborescens

PEA FAMILY

This large deciduous shrub or small tree was introduced into the region from Siberia and Manchuria for use as hedges and windbreaks, and it has naturalized in its new environment exceedingly well. It is a multi-stemmed shrub with erect to spreading branches that grows up to 5 m tall. The leaves are alternate, pinnately compound with eight to a dozen oval, entire, tipped leaflets. Its small yellow, pea-like flowers occur singly or in clusters. The fruits are slender, cylindrical legume pods that are brown to tan in colour.

Cushion Milk Vetch
Astragalus triphyllus

PEA FAMILY

This low-growing species forms dense mats of leaves and flower stems on the ground, and occurs on dry slopes and hillsides in prairies, coulees and eroded ground. The leaves are compound, with three elliptical leaflets, and they are thickly clustered around the base. The leaves and stems are densely covered with soft, silvery hairs, giving the plant a greyish-green hue. The flowers are yellowish-white with a purplish tint on the keel, and occur in short-stemmed clusters. The distinguishing feature of this species is its three-parted leaves.

Field Locoweed
Oxytropis campestris

PEA FAMILY

This early-blooming plant is widespread and common along roadsides and in rocky outcrops and dry open woods in the region. Its leaves are mainly basal, with elliptical leaflets and dense hairs. The pale-yellow, pea-like flowers bloom in clusters at the top of a leafless, hairy stem. The plant is poisonous to cattle, sheep and horses, owing to its high content of alkaloids that cause blind staggers. This loss of muscle control in animals that have ingested this plant is the origin of the common name for the flower, *loco* being Spanish for "crazy" or "foolish."

Yellow Hedysarum
Hedysarum sulphurescens

PEA FAMILY

This is a plant of stream banks, grasslands, open forests and clearings. Its yellowish to nearly white flowers are pea-like and drooping, usually appearing along one side of the stem in elongated clusters (racemes). The fruits of the plant are long, flat, pendulous pods with conspicuous winged edges and constrictions between each of the seeds. This plant is also called Yellow Sweet Vetch. It is an extremely important food for bears, which eat the roots in the spring and fall.

Yellow Sweet Clover
Melilotus officinalis

PEA FAMILY

This species was introduced as a forage plant for livestock, and it is now common on roadsides and embankments and in ditches and pastures. It grows to over 2 m in height, with smooth, leafy, branched stems. The leaflets are slightly toothed, and appear in threes. The yellow flowers bloom in long, narrow, tapered clusters at the top of the plant and in the leaf axils. Each individual flower has a typical pea shape. The plant contains coumarin, which imparts an overwhelmingly sweet fragrance when cut for hay.

Agrimony
Agrimonia striata

ROSE FAMILY

This erect, brownish perennial grows to over 1 m tall along roadsides and in open woods, thickets and clearings. Its leaves are pinnately divided into 7–11 lance-shaped, toothed, hairy major leaflets, with smaller leaflets often occurring between the major ones. The leaves are dark green and have tiny, stalkless glands beneath. The small, bright-yellow flowers have five petals and occur in dense, long, narrow, interrupted clusters at the top of the stem. The fruits are dry, cup-shaped achenes with hooked prickles that adhere to passersby and animals. The plant has long been used medicinally.

Early Cinquefoil

Potentilla concinna

ROSE FAMILY

This species is a very short, spreading perennial that supports two to five flowers per plant. The flowers are bright yellow, with five rounded petals, appearing as solitary flowers atop a leafless stem. The plant is usually less than 10 cm tall and blooms early in the spring, usually in dry, sandy soil. Indeed, it is often one of the first flowers seen in the spring.

Shrubby Cinquefoil

Potentilla fruticosa

ROSE FAMILY

This low deciduous shrub is found on rocky slopes and in dry meadows and gravelly river courses at low to subalpine elevations. Its leaves are alternate, divided into three to seven (usually five) greyish-green leaflets that are lightly hairy and often have curled edges. The flowers are golden yellow and saucer-shaped, with five rounded petals, usually blooming as a solitary at the end of branches. The flowers are often smaller and paler at lower elevations, larger and brighter at higher elevations. Many *Potentilla* species have five leaflets and the flower parts are in fives.

Narrow-Petalled Stonecrop (Wormleaf Stonecrop)

Sedum stenopetalum

STONECROP FAMILY

This low, erect perennial grows up to 15 cm tall in rocky and gravelly areas and grasslands. The leaves are alternate, brownish-green and succulent, often overlapping. The star-shaped yellow flowers have four to five lance-shaped petals, and occur in clusters at the top of the stem. Each flower has numerous yellow stamens. Some authorities say the plant is edible, while others disagree.

Jewelweed (Touch-Me-Not)

Impatiens noli-tangere

TOUCH-ME-NOT FAMILY

This plant is an annual that grows up to 150 cm tall in moist, shady poplar woods and thickets and along streams and lake margins. The plant is succulent and leafy. Its alternate, simple, ovate leaves are irregularly toothed and up to 12 cm long. The irregularly shaped flowers occur mostly in pairs from the upper leaf axils. The flowers are pale yellow with red or purple flecks, and consist of a sac-like dilated sepal that gradually narrows into a down-curved spur about 1 cm long. The plant releases seeds explosively when touched.

Yellow Wood Violet
Viola glabella

VIOLET FAMILY

This beautiful yellow violet occurs in moist woods, often in extensive patches. There are smooth, serrate, heart-shaped leaves on the upper part of the plant stem. The flowers have very short spurs, and the interior of the side petals often exhibits a white beard. The flower is also commonly referred to as Smooth Violet and Stream Violet.

Yellow Pond Lily (Yellow Water Lily)
Nuphar variegatum

WATER LILY FAMILY

This aquatic perennial found in ponds, lakes and slow-moving streams is perhaps the most recognizable water plant in the region. It grows from a thick rootstock, producing cord-like stems. The floating leaves, up to 15 cm long, are borne singly on long stems. They are waxy on the surface, round and broadly oval, and heart-shaped at the base. The large flowers protrude from the water's surface, as solitary on a long stalk.

GLOSSARY

achene: A dry, single-seeded fruit that does not split open at maturity.

alternate: A reference to the arrangement of leaves on a stem where the leaves appear singly and staggered on opposite sides of the stem.

annual: A plant that completes its life cycle, from seed germination to production of new seed, within one year and then dies.

anther: The portion of the stamen (the male portion of a flower) that produces pollen.

axil: The upper angle formed where a leaf, branch or other organ is attached to a plant stem.

basal: A reference to leaves that occur at the bottom of the plant, usually near or on the ground.

berry: A fleshy, many-seeded fruit.

biennial: A plant that completes its life cycle in two years, normally producing leaves in the first year and flowers in the second, before dying.

blade: The body of a leaf, excluding the stalk.

bract: A reduced or otherwise modified leaf that is usually found near the flower of a plant but is not part of the flower. *See also* **florescence**; **inflorescence**.

bulb: An underground plant part derived from a short, often rounded shoot that is covered with scales or leaves.

calyx: The outer set of flower parts, usually composed of sepals.

capsule: A dry fruit with more than one compartment that splits open to release seeds.

clasping: In reference to a leaf that surrounds or partially wraps around a stem or branch.

composite inflorescence: A flower-like **inflorescence** of the Composite Family, made up of **ray flowers** and/or **disc flowers**. Where both ray and disc flowers exist, the ray flowers surround the disc flowers.

compound leaf: A leaf that is divided into two or many leaflets, each of which may look like a complete leaf but lacks buds. Compound leaves may have a variety of arrangements.

connate: In reference to leaves where two leaves are fused at their bases to form a shallow cup, often seen in the Honeysuckle Family.

corm: An enlarged base or stem resembling a bulb.

corolla: The collective term for the petals of the flower that are found inside the sepals.

cultivar: A cultivated variety of a wild plant.

cyme: A broad, flat-topped flower arrangement in which the inner, central flowers bloom first.

decumbent: In reference to a plant reclining, or lying on the ground with tip ascending.

disc flower: Any of the small tubular florets found in the central, clustered portion of the flower head of members of the Composite Family; also referred to as "disc florets."

dioecious: Having unisex flowers, where male and female flowers appear on separate plants. *See also* **monoecious**.

drupe: A fleshy or juicy fruit that covers a single, stony seed inside, e.g., a cherry or a peach.

drupelet: Any one part of an aggregate fruit (like a raspberry or blackberry), where each such part is a fleshy fruit that covers a single, stony seed inside.

elliptical: Ellipse-shaped, widest in the middle. *See also* **oval**.

elongate: Having a slender form, long in relation to width.

entire: In reference to a leaf edge that is smooth, without teeth or notches.

filament: The part of the stamen that supports the anther. Also can refer to any threadlike structure.

florescence: Generally the flowering part of a plant; the arrangement of the flowers on the stem; also referred to as **inflorescence**. *But see* **bract**.

floret: One of the small tubular flowers in the central, clustered portion of the flower head of members of the Composite Family; also known as **disc flower**.

follicle: A dry fruit composed of a single compartment that splits open along one side at maturity to release seeds.

fruit: The ripe ovary with the enclosed seeds, and any other structures that enclose it.

glabrous: In reference to a leaf surface, smooth, neither waxy or sticky.

gland: A small organ that secretes a sticky or oily substance and is attached to some part of the plant.

glaucous: Having a fine, waxy, often white coating that may be rubbed off; often characteristic of leaves, fruits and stems.

hood: in reference to flower structure, a curving or folded petal-like structure interior to the petals and exterior to the stamens in certain flowers.

host: In reference to a parasitic or semi-parasitic plant, the plant from which the parasite obtains its nourishment.

inflorescence: Generally the flowering part of a plant; the arrangement of the flowers on the stem; also referred to as **florescence**. *But see* **bract**.

keel: The two fused petals in flowers that are members of the Pea Family.

lance-shaped: In reference to leaf shape, much longer than wide, widest below the middle and tapering to the tip, like the blade of a lance.

leaflet: A distinct, leaflike segment of a compound leaf.

linear: Like a line; long, narrow and parallel-sided.

lobe: A reference to the arrangement of leaves, a segment of a divided plant part, typically rounded.

margin: The edge of a leaf or petal.

mat: A densely interwoven or tangled, low, ground-hugging growth.

midrib: The main rib of a leaf.

mid-vein : The middle vein of a leaf.

monoecious: A plant having unisex flowers, with separate male and female flowers on the same plant. *See also* **dioecious**.

nectary: A plant structure that produces and secretes nectar.

node: A joint on a stem or root.

noxious weed: A plant, usually imported, that out-competes and drives out native plants.

oblong: Somewhat rectangular, with rounded ends.

obovate: Shaped like a teardrop.

opposite: A reference to the arrangement of leaves on a stem where the leaves appear paired on opposite sides of the stem, directly across from each other.

oval: Broadly elliptical.

ovary: The portion of the flower where the seeds develop. It is usually a swollen area below the style and stigma.

ovate: Egg-shaped.

palmate: A reference to the arrangement of leaves on a stem where the leaves spread like the fingers on a hand, diverging from a central or common point.

panicle: A branched inflorescence that blooms from the bottom up.

pencilled: Marked with coloured lines, like the petals on Violets.

perennial: A plant that does not produce seeds or flowers until its second year of life, then lives for three or more years, usually flowering each year before dying.

petal: A component of the inner floral portion of a flower, often the most brightly coloured and visible part of the flower.

petiole: The stem of a leaf.

pinnate: A reference to the arrangement of leaves on a stem where the leaves appear in two rows on opposite sides of a central stem, similar to the construction of a feather.

pistil: The female member of a flower that produces seed, consisting of the ovary, the style and the stigma. A flower may have one to several separate pistils.

pistillate: A flower with female reproductive parts but no male reproductive parts.

pollen: The tiny, often powdery male reproductive microspores formed in the stamens and necessary for sexual reproduction in flowering plants.

pome: A fruit with a core, e.g., an apple or pear.

prickle: A small, sharp, spiny outgrowth from the outer surface.

raceme: A flower arrangement that has an elongated flower cluster with the flowers attached to short stalks of relatively equal length that are attached to the main central stalk.

ray flower: One of the outer, strap-shaped petals seen in members of the Composite Family. Ray flowers may surround disc flowers or may comprise the whole of the flower head; also referred to as **ray florets**.

reflexed: Bent backwards, often in reference to petals, bracts or stalks.

rhizome: An underground stem that produces roots and shoots at the nodes.

rosette: A dense cluster of basal leaves from a common underground part, often in a flattened, circular arrangement.

runner: A long, trailing or creeping stem.

saprophyte: An organism that obtains its nutrients from dead organic matter.

scape: A flowering stem, usually leafless, rising from the crown, roots or corm of a plant. Scapes can have a single or many flowers.

sepal: A leaf-like appendage that surrounds the petals of a flower. Collectively the sepals make up the calyx.

serrate: Possessing sharp, forward-pointing teeth.

sessile: Of a plant structure attached directly by its base without a stalk; opposite of "stalked."

shrub: A multi-stemmed woody plant.

simple leaf: A leaf that has a single leaf-like blade, which may be lobed or divided.

spadix: A floral spike with a fleshy or succulent axis usually enclosed in a **spathe**.

spathe: A sheathing **bract** or pair of bracts partly enclosing an **inflorescence** and especially a **spadix** on the same axis.

spike: An elongated, unbranched cluster of stalkless or nearly stalkless flowers.

spine: A thin, stiff, sharp-pointed projection.

spur: A hollow, tubular projection arising from the base of a petal or sepal, often producing nectar.

stalk: The stem supporting the leaf, flower or flower cluster.

stamen: The male member of the flower, which produces pollen; the structure typically consists of an anther and a filament.

staminate: A flower with male reproductive parts but no female reproductive parts

staminode: A sterile stamen.

standard: The uppermost petal of a typical flower in the Pea Family.

stigma: The portion of the pistil receptive to pollination; usually at the top of the style and often sticky or fuzzy.

stolon: A creeping above-ground stem capable of sending up a new plant.

style: A slender stalk connecting the stigma to the ovary in the female organ of a flower.

taproot: A stout main root that extends downward.

tendril: A slender, coiled or twisted filament with which climbing plants attach to their supports.

tepals: Petals and sepals that cannot be distinguished, one from the other.

terminal: At the top of, such as of a stem or other appendage.

terminal flower head: A flower that appears at the top of a stem, as opposed to originating from a leaf axil.

ternate: Arranged in threes, often in reference to leaf structures.

toothed: Bearing teeth or sharply angled projections along the edge.

trailing: Lying flat on the ground but not rooting.

tuber: A thick, creeping underground stem.

tubular: Hollow or cylindrical, usually in reference to a fused corolla.

umbel: A flower arrangement where the flower stalks have a common point of attachment to the stem, like the spokes of an umbrella.

unisexual: Some flowers are unisexual, having either male parts or female parts but not both. Some plants are unisexual, having either male flowers or female flowers but not both.

urn-shaped: Hollow and cylindrical or globular, contracted at the mouth; like an urn.

vacuole: A membrane-bound compartment in a plant that is typically filled with liquid and may perform various functions in the plant.

vein: A small tube that carries water, nutrients and minerals, usually referring to leaves.

viscid: Sticky, thick and gluey.

whorl: Three or more parts attached at the same point along a stem or axis, often surrounding the stem; forming a ring radiating out from a common point.

wings: Side petals that flank the keel in typical flowers of the Pea Family.

INDEX

ABOUT THE AUTHOR

Neil Jennings is an ardent hiker, photographer and outdoorsman who loves "getting down in the dirt" pursuing his keen interest in wildflowers. For 22 years he co-owned a fly-fishing retail store in Calgary, and he has fly-fished extensively, in both fresh and saltwater, for decades. His angling pursuits usually lead him to wildflower investigations in a variety of locations. He taught fly-fishing-related courses in Calgary for over 20 years, and his photographs and writings on that subject have appeared in a number of outdoor magazines. Neil has previously written several volumes published by Rocky Mountain Books, dealing with wildflowers in western Canada, fly-fishing, and hiking venues in southern Alberta. He lives in Calgary, Alberta, with Linda, his wife of over 40 years. They spend a lot of time outdoors together chasing fish, flowers and, as often as possible, grandchildren.